HORATIO
NELSON

POCKET
GIANTS

HORATIO
NELSON

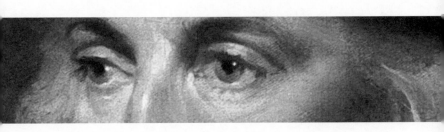

POCKET
GIANTS

PETER
WARWICK

Cover image © Bridgeman Images

First published 2015

The History Press
The Mill, Brimscombe Port
Stroud, Gloucestershire, GL5 2QG
www.thehistorypress.co.uk

British Library Cataloguing in Publication Data.
A catalogue record for this book is available from the British Library.

ISBN 978 0 7509 6266 7

Typesetting and origination by The History Press
Printed and bound in Malta, by Melita Press

Contents

Acknowledgements

Thank you to my very dear friends Ian and Pat Grimble, whose wonderful Devon home made this volume possible; to John Curtis and Tony Morris for reading and commenting on the manuscript; and to my marvellous son Tom, who continues to suffer Nelson!

Introduction

In Search of Nelson

Hope revives within me. I shall recover, and my dream of glory be fulfilled. Nelson will yet be an admiral.

Horatio Nelson, 1 September 1780[1]

At times during his career, Horatio Nelson seemed an unlikely candidate for greatness. For instance, at the end of 1776 he fell ill from malaria and was discharged from the navy. Four years later, at the height of a campaign in Central America, he was struck down again and had to be invalided home. In January 1782 his ship was severely damaged in a collision. In 1784 he was on half pay and ill in London. In 1787, as senior naval officer in the Leeward Islands, he mishandled a situation involving a fellow officer and future king, Prince William Henry, which put him out of favour with the Admiralty for five years. In July 1797 he led a disastrous and bloody attack on Santa Cruz de Tenerife and lost his right arm in the action. He himself concluded that his career was now at an end, writing, 'a left-handed admiral will never again be considered as useful'.[2] Two years later he was deeply embroiled in Sicilian politics, complicit in atrocities ashore, lampooned in the press for a scandalous relationship with another man's wife, reprimanded by the Admiralty and summoned home in ignominy. Earl St Vincent remarked, 'Nelson will never be fit for an independent command.'[3] In August 1801 he masterminded two abortive attacks on French gunboats at Boulogne. Finally, for two years between 1803 and 1805, he failed to bring the enemy to action.

The truth is that Nelson's extraordinary and often controversial career was not a smooth progression from midshipman to admiral; from boy to hero. He made many mistakes. His judgement was not always sound. He suffered reverses, some of which were of his own making.

There are many Nelsons, depending on which period and which aspect of his life is highlighted. The differences and contradictions are reflected in the many contemporary accounts and portraits of him – he sat for all the great artists of the day, save Sir Thomas Lawrence. The general perception is that of a frail man, 5ft 7in tall. His many injuries and complaints caused him to age prematurely: by 1800 his hair had turned white. In terms of personality, there is the young and earnest Nelson, often naive but already displaying flashes of originality; the more experienced Nelson with a solid reputation, eager for fame and glory yet humbled by his own hubris; the patriotic and dutiful Nelson; the Nelson imbued with both physical and moral courage. There is also the ruthless, fighting Nelson with a heart tempered by a strong sense of humanity and religious faith; the passionate lover, doting father and loyal friend; the sensitive, generous Nelson, thinking about and caring for others; and the charming, charismatic Nelson with a dry sense of humour and a 'sweet smile'. To these descriptions must be added the insecure, emotionally vulnerable and easily depressed Nelson, always striving for perfection whilst craving official recognition and popular acclaim; and, finally, the accomplished Nelson, who during the last two years of his life managed to distil all of these attributes and characteristics to achieve his goal.

To appreciate how he reached this apogee after such a fluctuating, even erratic, career we might reflect on the words which conclude his fragment of autobiography written in 1799:

> Thus may be exemplified by my life, that perseverance in any profession will most probably meet its reward. Without having any inheritance, or having been fortunate in prize money, I have received all the honours of my profession, been created a peer of Great Britain, and I may say to the reader, 'Go Thou and Do Likewise.'[4]

The key word is 'perseverance'. Nelson was driven by the need to achieve and rarely faltered in his attempts to do so. It might even be argued that perseverance was his star quality, since without it the full potential of his positive attributes may never have been realised.

Nevertheless, Nelson's illustrious naval career was only made possible by the coincidence of war during his lifetime; by 'interest', meaning influence in the right places; and by the fact that the Royal Navy was blessed with an elite of remarkably talented naval officers. Nelson has emerged as the icon for them all and for the naval service as a whole. He was the first to recognise their importance to his own achievements.

In spite of these advantages, there can be no doubting Nelson's ability to seize and even create decisive opportunities, for instance at the battles of Cape St Vincent and Copenhagen, and to act with originality.

However, Nelson's most exceptional attribute was not his strategic and tactical prowess, important though that was. It was his leadership style. In 1913 the British government commissioned a report into the tactics at Trafalgar. The expectation was that some elegant mathematical formula would explain the execution of Nelson's plan and that this could be replicated in a future battle. The inquiry missed the point completely by failing to recognise that it was Nelson's radical leadership style and the atmosphere that it created that was the secret to his success in battle.

During the course of his naval career, Nelson saw action on more than 120 occasions and sailed to many parts of the world, including the Mediterranean, India, Central and North America, the West Indies and the Arctic. His thirst for battle and hunger for glory often put others at risk, but only risks he himself was personally prepared to take. He demonstrated emphatically at his three outstanding victories, the Nile, Copenhagen and Trafalgar, that he not only took risks but could bring them off successfully.

Nelson was exceptionally good at communicating his ideas and plans to his officers, but in all his commands he also inspired confidence and created harmony. His leadership communicated the sense to his captains that they could do things without waiting for permission from him. In return, he conveyed that he could rely on their initiative to follow through as a battle evolved. This was unusual amongst eighteenth-century admirals, who rarely shared their ideas with fellow officers. Moreover, his captains knew he would support their own risk-taking afterwards, no matter the outcome. This empowerment was the key essence of Nelson the Leader rather than Nelson the Commander. It is what differentiates him from, say, the Duke of Wellington, who, in spite of his deserved and illustrious reputation, was a great commander rather than an authentic leader. A lieutenant in the 30th Foot once wrote of Wellington: 'No leader ever possessed so fully the confidence of his soldiers, but none did love him.'[5] Criticised for being cold and aloof throughout his career, Wellington never inspired the adulation from his soldiers that Nelson gained from his sailors.

Nelson learnt from his predecessors from an early age. Talk of Admiral Sir Edward Hawke's pursuit of a large French fleet into the tempestuous Quiberon Bay on 20 November 1759 would have been captivating stuff for an adventurous boy, especially as his maternal uncle was a prominent sailor himself, who told the Nelson children stirring stories of his adventures in the Seven Years War. Nelson was impressed by Hawke's aggression and decisiveness, which he came to emulate, not least at the Battle of the Nile, where he pounced on the French fleet at anchor in Aboukir Bay as the sun was setting, echoing Hawke's own headlong pursuit at Quiberon.

The hero whom Nelson most admired was Major-General James Wolfe, who was killed, aged 32, during his victorious attack on Quebec, also in 1759. On seeing Benjamin West's famous painting of the death scene, Nelson asked the artist to paint his own, should he be killed in action, which West did.

In order to appreciate Nelson's exceptional career it is also essential to understand the role that the Royal Navy played in eighteenth-century British society, politically, economically and socially, and how it had gained such importance. The British economy was growing as a result of improvements in agricultural productivity and increasing colonial foreign trade, especially with the East Indies. This created an investment surplus that allowed the government to borrow large sums at low rates of interest through a sophisticated financial system first established in the late seventeenth century to meet the needs of war with France. Foreign trade was protected by the navy and was, through taxation, the means to pay for it; a formula which was willingly approved by the population. This gave Britain a huge advantage over France and Spain and placed the Royal Navy at the heart of the national project. The British people saw that it was sea power that protected their country from foreign invasion. It guaranteed their freedom and preserved their liberties, and provided the long-term security that allowed the economy to grow. It was a virtuous circle. War created the demand that was the ultimate stimulus for that growth.

At the time of Nelson's birth in 1758 the Royal Navy consisted of more than 400 ships, making it the strongest naval force in the world. This fleet was supported by the globe's largest industrial complex, with great dockyards employing tens of thousands, and a highly sophisticated and effective administrative bureaucracy, out of which grew today's Civil Service. The navy had benefited from the recent successes of the Seven Years War, particularly in gaining the ability to keep fleets at sea for long periods, escorting convoys and blockading enemy ports. This had given it a margin of superiority over the navies of France and Spain, and a belief in victory. Typically, its sailors were fit, well trained and disciplined. Discipline was regulated and could be harsh, but generally sailors enjoyed a relationship with their officers based on a tradition of tolerance and humanity which harked back to the Elizabethan age. Moreover, because the parliamentary system had gained control of the navy in the late seventeenth century, sailors were regarded favourably by the people as an expression of their liberty, unlike soldiers – the army was suspected as a manifestation of the power of the Crown.

In revolutionary times this was a profound factor. It allowed good sea officers to command their men through motivation and trust. Nelson recognised this phenomenon very early on in his career and, once it was blended with his own ease, openness and instinctive ability to mix with people of every social background, created the atmosphere that set him on the course that made him a natural leader. Moreover, he was affectionate, kind and generous to those who pleased or served him well. Nelson was a loyal friend. If anyone helped him, he never forgot it and always sought to repay the favour. He encouraged promising young officers and assisted them in their careers, especially if they were sons of people who had helped him when he was young.

'Interest' was crucial to the early stages of Nelson's career; indeed, it was so for any young officer making his way in the eighteenth-century Royal Navy. The navy, however, was a service that also required merit, and

Nelson's achievement goes way beyond what 'interest' alone could deliver. This was his doing, no one else's. Moreover, because he came from 'middling stock' rather than aristocracy, he displayed none of the patrician characteristics of that class, typical of so many army officers, including the Duke of Wellington. This class difference was the bedrock of his ordinariness, the quality which made him so accessible to those serving with and below him. While he valued the trappings of status, he always wore them with a degree of nonchalance as well as self-satisfaction and pride.

A recent examination by Mackay and Duffy of the qualities which made for successful naval leadership during the Golden Age of the Royal Navy between 1740 and 1815 identified twelve key qualities. It judges admirals, including Anson, Duncan, Hawke, Hood, Howe, Jervis, Keppel, Nelson, Rodney and Vernon, in terms of those attributes. It concludes that only two naval leaders of the eighteenth century exemplified all twelve qualities: Edward Hawke and Horatio Nelson. The leadership characteristics examined were: originality; seamanship; bravery and aggression; tactical flair; planning; grasp of strategy; moral courage allied to excellence of judgement; personal leadership; clarity of communication; zealous concern for the effect of the commanding admiral's conduct on the morale, effectiveness and cohesion of the service as a whole; a major victory, conclusive in the naval theatre of the war in question; and physical stamina.

Edward Hawke is hardly known. His career has been greatly undervalued, whereas Nelson's fame burns as brightly as ever. It may simply be the case that Hawke lacked Nelson's peculiar personal charm and rare ability to appear as both an ordinary man and a superman at the same time. There is undoubtedly something about Nelson, an elusive piece of magic, which makes him exceptional.

In August 1805 the First Lord of the Admiralty, Lord Barham, had to decide whether the 46-year-old Vice Admiral Lord Nelson was the right senior officer to command a fleet that would sail from England to do battle with the combined fleets of France and Spain. It was not a straightforward decision. Nelson was a complex character and he had spent the last two years, in his own words, 'playing cat and mouse' with the French but had failed to bring them to battle.[6] It looked to some as if he was guilty of misjudgement, as he appeared to have allowed the French to escape from the Mediterranean and link up with Spanish warships.

Nelson himself was frustrated. Writing to Lady Hamilton, he fretted, 'Your poor, dear Nelson is, my dearest beloved Emma, very, very unwell. After a two years' fag. It has been mortifying the not being able to get at the enemy.'[7] On his return to Portsmouth he could not be confident that either the Admiralty or the public would still favour him. Might this be yet another, possibly final, setback to his ambition to be a hero, robbing him of his destiny?

Lord Barham, sitting in the oak-panelled boardroom of the Admiralty in Whitehall, was able to cast a long and thoughtful eye over Nelson's life and career. He could study Nelson's sea journals, orders, commands and correspondence over the last two years to understand the admiral's reasoning and to see why he had not brought the French to battle. He needed to reassure himself that Nelson was not just a risk-taking maverick prone to making mistakes. Looking at Nelson's career as a whole, he would find extraordinary moments that showed Nelson to be a great fighting admiral, but he would also find times when Nelson's discipline and judgement appeared suspect and his risk-taking looked nothing less than reckless. Barham's conclusion was the same as that reached by his predecessor the Earl St Vincent, who had been First Lord of the Admiralty from 1801 to 1804: 'I never saw a man in our profession who possessed the magic art of infusing the same spirit into others which inspired their own actions, exclusive of other talents and habits of business not common to naval officers … All agree there is but one Nelson.'[8]

1

A Norfolk Childhood

Let them alone. Little Horace will beat them!

Mrs Catherine Nelson (attributed)[9]

Horatio Nelson was born seven weeks early, on 29 September 1758, in the parsonage house at Burnham Thorpe in north Norfolk. His father, the Reverend Edmund Nelson, was rector of the parish. Although his mother Catherine was proud to be the great-niece of Sir Robert Walpole, Britain's first prime minister, his background was by no means grand – he described himself as belonging to a 'middling class of people'.[10] He was christened Horatio after Walpole's son, but to his family he was always known as 'Horace'. There were seven other surviving children in the family and, throughout his life, Nelson appears to have been happiest when surrounded by his siblings. He was at heart a family man and his family was an important source of inner strength.

Life was not easy, especially when his generous, fun-loving and strong-willed mother died on Boxing Day 1767. Her death left the 9-year-old boy emotionally insecure and vulnerable. In middle age he was to say, 'the thought of former days brings all my mother into my heart, which shows itself in my eyes.'[11] Eventually, after three lonely years, he decided he would like to go to sea, possibly seeing the navy as a substitute for the love and domesticity that had died with Catherine. He asked his brother William to write to their maternal uncle, the brave and urbane Captain Maurice Suckling RN, asking him to take the boy aboard with him. Suckling wrote back, 'What has poor little Horace done, who is so weak, that he above all the rest should be sent to rough it at sea? But let him come, and the first time we go into action a cannon ball may knock off his head and provide for him at once.'[12]

There are many tales about 'little Horace', but we have to be very wary of their veracity, since they can frequently be attributed to the vivid imagination of his elder brother William and to his early hagiographers, such as James Stanier Clarke and John McArthur, whose *The Life of Admiral Lord Nelson* was published four years after his death. It is as if they were compelled to show that from his earliest days there was something special about Nelson. Three of the tales are, however, worth retelling.

Nelson, aged 5, had gone off alone bird's-nesting and failed to return home on time. His anxious family went in search of him. He was found under a hedge, happily admiring his day's collection of eggs. His angry grandmother said she was surprised fear had not driven him home, to which Nelson is supposed to have replied, 'Madam, I never saw *fear*!'[13]

In January 1770, Nelson, now aged 11, set off with his elder brother, William, to boarding school in North Walsham, some 40 miles away. They were stopped by snowdrifts and came back home. Their father, a strict disciplinarian, admonished them and insisted they try again, this time leaving it to their 'honour' to return only if they found it 'dangerous'. William was all for giving up but

Horatio stiffened his resolve with the words, 'Remember, brother. It was left to our honour!'[14]

At Paston School in North Walsham there was a large pear tree close to the schoolhouse. Nelson's classmates lowered him on knotted sheets from the dormitory window into the tree. He picked as many pears as he could and, when safely back inside, handed them to his friends, keeping none for himself. Nelson claimed, 'I took them because every other boy was afraid!'[15] In spite of a large reward, none of them informed on him.

Paston School was the second Nelson attended, the first being the Royal Grammar School in Norwich. It was comparatively new and its curriculum was more liberal than was typical at the time. Boys were taught French as well as the Classics. Nelson appears to have enjoyed Shakespeare's plays and often quoted or paraphrased lines from them in his later letters. *Henry V* was clearly his favourite. Here is the story of a great leader, visionary yet pragmatic, powerful yet responsible. Henry V was Nelson's unwitting guide to the reality of tough decision-making and courageous personal challenge.

Nelson's boyhood experience gave him another crucial attribute. It was one that would guide and influence him for the rest of his life: religious faith. Nelson had an early introduction to religion. He assisted his father at the altar of All Saints' church, Burnham Thorpe, where he even stood as godfather at baptisms. Every night and morning of his life, Nelson knelt in prayer, developing a faith that seldom referred to Jesus Christ or the Trinity. He believed in predestination or providence. It was as if he had a direct line to God.

In his private journal in 1791, he wrote, 'When I lay me down to sleep I recommend myself to the care of Almighty God, and when I awaken I give myself up to His direction amidst all the evils that threaten me.' In one of his letters to Emma Hamilton, composed shortly after the Battle of Copenhagen in 1801, he wrote, 'I own myself a *believer in God*, and if I have any merit in not fearing death, it is because I feel that I must fall whenever it is His good pleasure.'[16]

For the thirty-four years of his naval life, his soaring ambition for glory and honour was complemented by a genuine humility before the Almighty.

2

Learning the Ropes

Firstly you must always implicitly obey orders, without attempting to form any opinion of your own regarding their propriety. Secondly, you must consider every man your enemy who speaks ill of your king; and thirdly you must hate a Frenchman as you hate the devil.

Horatio Nelson, 1793[17]

The timing was perfect. In 1770, when William Nelson wrote on his brother's behalf to Captain Maurice Suckling, their uncle had recently been appointed to the command of His Majesty's Ship *Raisonnable*, a 64-gun third-rate battleship of the line recently brought into service because of a threatened war with Spain over the ownership of the Falkland Islands. Suckling invited his 12-year-old nephew to join the ship at the royal dockyard at Chatham. The entry in the *Raisonnable*'s muster book for 24 April 1771 records, 'Horace Nelson, Midshipman'. Nelson's extreme youth was typical for the time. It must, nevertheless, have been a tremendous shock for him to move suddenly from the quiet rural life of a Norfolk coastal village to the cramped, crowded, dark and dangerous world of an eighteenth-century warship, with sights, sounds and smells all unfamiliar to him, and doubly so since his uncle was not there to greet him. Nelson spent his first few days in this strange wooden world alone and homesick.

His stay in *Raisonnable* was short lived: the Falklands crisis abated. Suckling wisely removed his nephew to a merchantman, the *Mary Ann*, for sea experience. The episode had one unintended consequence, which Nelson described:

I returned a practical seaman, with a horror of the Royal Navy, and with a saying then constant with the seamen, 'Aft the most honour, forward the better man!' It was many weeks before I got in the least reconciled to a man-of-war, so deep was the prejudice rooted, and what pains were taken to instill this erroneous principle in a young mind.[18]

It was a raw experience but it had a beneficial impact on the evolution of Nelson's leadership style.

He returned to the naval service because, being a structured service, it offered a hierarchy for promotion and, more importantly for Nelson, the opportunity for glory and heroism. The success of his apprenticeship, nevertheless, rested upon 'interest' – and this meant the support of Maurice Suckling. He seems to have planned a variety of experiences for his nephew, including keeping him out of the big ships of the line, so that the young Nelson's independent spirit could have free rein, giving his individuality every opportunity to assert itself.

Nelson's aim, as with all midshipmen, was to complete the six years of sea service which would then allow him to sit for his lieutenant's exam – a critical and essential step in any young officer's naval career. Nelson needed to be a practical seaman if he was to rise to the top of his profession. In the Royal Navy this skill came before social respectability. It meant 'learning the ropes' in order to acquire all-round competence in boat and ship handling; inshore, coastal and ocean navigation; weather and sea conditions; and all the activities of an able seaman. This technical knowledge was the basis for respect when assuming the responsibility of command: Nelson could always claim that he had done whatever he asked others to do.

Nelson's earliest experience of command came at the age of 14 when he was put in charge of a ship's boat near Chatham with a crew of fifteen grown men. The waters of the Thames Estuary became very familiar to him. The experience made him 'confident of myself amongst rocks and sands, which has many times since been of great comfort to me', as the battles of the Nile and Copenhagen, both fought in shoals, were to show.[19] Thorough practice was the key to success, and Suckling's interest ensured that Nelson was placed on voyages to the Arctic, the Indian Ocean and the West Indies.

The Arctic was Nelson's first real taste of adventure. This was the age of exploration and in 1773 an expedition, commanded by Commodore Constantine Phipps, set sail under the joint auspices of the navy and the Royal Society. Two bomb vessels, *Racehorse* and *Carcass*, were fitted out in an attempt to reach the North Pole. It would be a risky voyage and Phipps was ordered to recruit only 'effective men'. Such a request would seem to preclude a boy of 14. Nelson's uncle lied, however, about his nephew's age. Also, according to Nelson, 'I fancied I was to fill a man's place. I begged to be his coxswain,' to which, 'finding my ardent desire for going with him', the captain of the *Carcass*, Skeffington Lutwidge, agreed. Later Nelson was to write that he had been given charge of the *Carcass*'s four-oared cutter and twelve crew, 'and prided myself in fancying I could navigate her better than any other boat in the ship'.[20]

The ice was particularly thick that summer and the ships only managed to get to 80° 48′ N, a little to the north-east of Spitzbergen. There they were held fast by the ice and were in real danger. For one moment it looked as if they would have to abandon the ships and take to the small boats, dragging them across the ice. Fortunately, the temperature rose and the ice loosened its grip, allowing the expedition to return to Great Yarmouth. Nelson had enjoyed a rare experience, fed his restless energy and boosted his seamanship skills and growing self-confidence. He had also had a brush with a polar bear!

The story of this encounter, on 4 August 1773, has become part of the Nelson legend. Surprisingly, Nelson makes no reference to it himself, nor does the ship's log record it, other than to say that 'a bear came close to the ship on the ice, but on the people's going towards him he went away'.[21] It was left to others to take the rudimentary facts of the tale, embroidering and exaggerating them as they saw fit, to highlight Nelson's bravery. There are many versions. They are all apocryphal, but the core version must be told. It seems that Nelson and another daring shipmate left the ship so that he could kill an approaching bear and get the skin for his father. Nelson's musket misfired but, ignoring the entreaties of his companion, he attempted to cross the chasm in the ice that separated them from their prey so that he could beat the bear to death with the butt end of his musket. They were spotted from the ship, through a swirling mist, and a signal gun was fired for them to return. The bear was frightened away and a despondent Nelson returned to face an angry Captain Lutwidge.

Within one week of returning from his six months in the Arctic, Nelson had been entered by his uncle Captain Suckling onto the books of the old 24-gun frigate *Seahorse*, commanded by Captain George Farmer and bound for a voyage to the East Indies via the Cape of Good Hope, the furthest and most exotic station maintained by the Royal Navy. Nelson was delighted. As well as the tales of Hawke and Wolfe, he had been raised on the romance of Clive of India's victories.

At sea for two years, he sailed the Indian Ocean, the Arabian Sea, the Straits of Hormuz and the Bay of Bengal, becoming familiar with places such as Bombay, Goa, Madras, Muscat and Trincomalee. It must have been an intoxicating experience for the teenage boy. It was also his introduction to the more brutal side of the Royal Navy. The *Seahorse* was not a happy ship, largely because her first lieutenant was a drunkard who often defied Captain Farmer's authority. He was eventually court-martialled and dismissed, but Nelson saw at first hand how a captain reliant on gratuitous punishment created an atmosphere of disharmony. In less than two years there were nearly a hundred floggings. Brutality was no substitute for strong leadership. Nelson kept out of trouble and was complimented on his sailing abilities. He even saw action for the first time when, on 19 February 1775, the *Seahorse* intercepted, fired on and eventually boarded two enemy ketches chasing a British East Indiaman.

One year later, now aged 18, Nelson fell dangerously ill with malaria and had to be invalided back to England. He had lost the use of his limbs, was emaciated and hovered between life and death. It was during the five-month voyage home in the leaking *Dolphin* that he underwent what can be best described as a quasi-spiritual experience which brought him back from the brink. He claimed to have been visited by a 'radiant orb' which brought a feeling of exultation. In his words:

> I felt impressed with an idea that I should never rise in my profession. My mind was staggered with a view of the difficulties I had to surmount and the little 'interest' I possessed. I could discover no means of reaching the object of my ambition. After a long and gloomy reverie, in which I almost wished myself overboard, a sudden glow of patriotism was kindled within me, and presented my king and country as my patron. My mind exulted in the idea. 'Well then,' I exclaimed, 'I *will* be a hero, and confiding in Providence, I will brave every danger.'[22]

Thereafter he was fearless for his own fate.

The "little 'interest'" was there ready to help him once again. Suckling, who had also advanced in the service and was now Comptroller of the Navy, placed Nelson as acting lieutenant aboard the 64-gun *Worcester*, so that he could complete his sea time and go on to sit his lieutenant's exam. This he did, successfully, on 5 April 1777. Nelson was now a professional sailor.

Suckling had done a good job. In four years his protégé had sailed 45,000 miles, gained a wide range of experiences in many different ships and locations, seen action and danger, suffered loneliness and the tedium of long sea voyages and had been required to use his initiative on an almost daily basis. The experience had encouraged Nelson's independence, energy and ambition and deepened his awareness of the fundamentals of leadership.

The next step was to make captain. This he achieved just three months short of his twenty-first birthday on 1 September 1779. The intervening two years were formative. Nelson was commissioned initially as second lieutenant of the *Lowestoffe*, a crack 32-gun frigate on the West Indies station during the War of American Independence. It was commanded by the well-read and knowledgeable William Locker, who bore the injuries of hand-to-hand fighting and had been with Hawke at Quiberon Bay in 1759. Hawke's dash, confidence and aggression had determined Locker's own naval philosophy, which he now passed on to the receptive and impressionable Nelson. They served together for only thirteen months, but remained close friends afterwards. Locker's influence on Nelson as a fighting man was seminal. As Nelson wrote lovingly to him many years later following his stunning victory at the Nile:

You, my old friend, after twenty-seven years acquaintance know that nothing can alter my attachment and gratitude to you. I have been your scholar. It is you who taught me to board a Frenchman, by your conduct … It is you who always told, 'Lay a Frenchman close, and you will beat him', and my only merit in my profession is being a good scholar. Our friendship will never end but with my life.[23]

Within a year Locker had given Nelson command of the small schooner which acted as the *Lowestoffe*'s tender. Less than a year later he was promoted to master and commander, which entitled him to his first independent command, even if it was only of the tiny, worn-out, armed brig *Badger*. In it he cruised the Caribbean and at one point oversaw the defence of Kingston, Jamaica, which was threatened by the French fleet under Admiral d'Estaing.

Six months later Nelson was 'made post', achieving the rank of full captain and given command of a sixth-rate ship of the line, the 28-gun frigate *Hinchinbroke*. A lieutenant held the courtesy title of captain if in command of an unrated ship but, on being given command of a rated ship, he was made post captain. Promotion would now follow automatically and, being young, Nelson could expect eventually to become an admiral by virtue of seniority on the list, irrespective of ability. He had been promoted over the heads of more senior colleagues. Moreover, he had served as lieutenant for less than three years and had not been absorbed into the strict hierarchy of the wardroom. His natural independence still had free rein.

Sadly, Maurice Suckling never witnessed his nephew's achievement, which he had done so much to help bring about. He died in July 1777. Nelson was now without 'interest' and would have to make his own way.

3

Frigate Captain

Hope revives within me. I shall recover, and my dream of glory be fulfilled. Nelson will yet be an admiral. It is the climate that has destroyed my health and crushed my spirits. Home, and dear friends, will restore me.

Horatio Nelson, 1 September 1780[24]

Nelson was destined to spend the next eight years almost continuously in command of frigates. Meanwhile, the ravages of life on the West Indies station were beginning to take their toll and he was experiencing his '*old* complaint in my breast',[25] which was almost certainly a continuing attack of malaria. His doctors advised him to return to England, but Nelson was impatient for action and looked to his commander-in-chief, Admiral Sir Peter Parker, for patronage. Parker, who had already overseen Nelson's promotion and his command of the *Badger*, took him under his wing. They became lifelong friends, with Parker serving as chief mourner at Nelson's funeral.

In 1780 Britain was at war with America and was also fighting France and Spain, which had allied themselves with the Americans. There were a number of major fleet actions, including Virginia Capes, a defeat for the British which presaged the loss of Yorktown and, subsequently, the American colonies. This was balanced by Admiral Rodney's victory over the French at the Battle of the Saintes, where he broke the line. Nelson missed out on these, but instead found himself the highest-ranking officer on a small-scale amphibious expedition against the Spanish Fort San Juan in modern-day Nicaragua.

The plan was to strike at the Spanish mainland and open a way for a British naval presence in the Pacific in order to threaten the Spanish west coast. Nelson's orders were to disembark the soldiers only; but, seeing their subsequent difficulties, he called for naval volunteers and offered his own support, helping the army to navigate the river to the fort and even assisting in the laying of guns. As the leader of the expedition Major Polson wrote, 'He was first upon every occasion, whether by day or by night, there was scarcely a gun fired but was pointed by him or Lieutenant Despard.'[26] Eventually the fort fell, but in reality the expedition had been a disaster. Only 380 of the 1,800 soldiers and sailors in the expedition survived – and Nelson was also struck down. The enemy, however, was not the Spanish defenders but dysentery, typhoid and malaria. Nelson languished in his tent for days until an order arrived from Parker to take command of another ship. This almost certainly saved his life. On reaching Port Royal, the emaciated Nelson was in no fit state to take command of anything. Instead he was cared for by the admiral and his wife until he was well enough to be invalided back to England.

A depressed Nelson might have been comforted had he had sight of Parker's report to the Admiralty. Impressed by Nelson's initiative, courage and, above all, leadership, Parker wrote, 'I wish much for his recovery. His abilities in his profession would be a loss to the service.'[27] Nelson's recovery in Bath was frustratingly slow and, as had happened earlier, he found that from time to time he seemed to lose the use of his left arm and left leg. Nonetheless, he petitioned the Admiralty for a ship. From beyond the grave his uncle once more came to his assistance. Charles Jenkinson, the Secretary at War, wrote to the First Lord of the Admiralty, Lord Sandwich, highlighting the fact that Nelson was the 'nephew of the late Comptroller of the Navy Mr Suckling and bears as I am assured a very good character'.[28]

4

America and the West Indies

Whilst I have the honour to command an English man-of-war, I never shall allow myself to be subservient to the will of any governor, nor cooperate with him in doing illegal acts.

Horatio Nelson, 1785[29]

Nearly a year passed before, in the autumn of 1781, Nelson secured the command of the 28-gun frigate *Albemarle*. She was not purpose-built, being a converted French prize, but Nelson was not complaining. 'Interest' had once again placed him ahead of others arguably more deserving. In letters to family and friends he praises the ship and crew. In his letter book and official correspondence, however, he reveals his dissatisfaction, describing his makeshift ship as sailing 'exceedingly crank'.[30] He had difficulty filling her complement and had to request the loan of forty Greenwich pensioners just to sail her downriver from Woolwich to the Nore. When at last assigned to convoy duty in the Baltic, he bemoaned the way 'very few of the ships paid the least regard to any signals'.[31] He also clashed in a manner bordering on insubordination with his fleet admiral, Sir Richard Hughes, over a missing anchor. This planted the seeds of a more unfortunate confrontation that would take place three years later. Bringing this unhappy tour to an end, the *Albemarle* was run down during a storm by a large merchantman and damaged seriously. Nelson remarked, 'we ought to be thankful we did not founder.'[32]

Three months later, and with his ship repaired, Nelson was posted to North America, calling first at Quebec.

Here he not only demonstrated his ability to take intelligent independent action against privateers harassing merchant ships on the St Lawrence River, but also came close to losing his heart to an attractive 23-year-old local belle, Mary Simpson, for whom it seems he was even prepared to give up his naval career. They had been introduced to each other by Alexander Davison, a merchant and businessman who eventually became Nelson's close friend and prize agent, collecting on his behalf profits arising from the sale of prizes, either cargo or vessels. It was Davison who convinced the besotted Nelson that, if he proposed to Miss Simpson, 'utter ruin ... must inevitably follow'[33] – meaning the loss of his career in the Royal Navy.

Nelson left Quebec for New York, where he joined Admiral Lord Hood's squadron. Even though the war with America was winding down, he broke away from the squadron to capture a French merchantman worth £20,000 as a prize, but Hood ruled that this money should be shared throughout the squadron because it had been in sight of the action. In spite of this apparent unfairness, Nelson asked to be transferred to Hood's command in the Caribbean, where he felt there would still be opportunities for battle, glory and honour. Hood liked Nelson's spirit and agreed, knowing also that he had experience of Jamaica station.

As the Battle of the Saintes had knocked the stuffing out of the French in the Caribbean, the best opportunity Nelson could find for a fight was to lead an attack with several ships against the French-held Grand Turk Island off the coast of Haiti. Before attacking, Nelson called for the garrison's surrender, which was refused. He then waited until the following day before ordering a frontal attack, which was repulsed. With seven wounded he called off the attack so as not to take further losses. (With peace imminent, he decided sensibly that it was not worth the cost.) Nelson had thrown away the element of surprise. It was a salutary lesson, as was the need for intelligence, reconnaissance and detailed planning. These lessons were only partially heeded, as his abortive attack on Santa Cruz in Tenerife fourteen years later was to prove. An examination of these, his first operational orders, nevertheless reveals his prevailing aggressive streak: they direct his ships to 'batter the enemy's entrenchments ... till they are totally destroyed'.[34]

Lord Hood did not lose faith in Nelson as a result of the Grand Turk episode, and their relationship strengthened as the years went by. It was Hood who, in 1793, gave Nelson the third and defining chance to advance his career. Nelson described Hood as 'certainly the best officer I ever saw. Everything from him is so clear it is impossible to misunderstand him.'[35]

While in New York, Hood introduced Nelson to His Royal Highness Prince William Henry, later Duke of Clarence and then King William IV, who was serving as a midshipman on board his flagship. It was an acquaintance that brought mixed blessings to Nelson and sparked an incident that would put Nelson's career on hold for five years. The prince recorded his first impressions of Nelson. They are an amusing and rare glimpse of this still young, incongruous, rather idiosyncratic figure:

I ... had the watch on deck, when Captain Nelson of the *Albemarle* came in his barge alongside, who appeared to be the merest boy of a captain I ever beheld, and his dress was worthy of attention. He had on a full-laced uniform. His lank unpowdered hair was tied in a stiff hessian tail of an extraordinary length. The old-fashioned flaps of his waistcoat added to the general quaintness of his figure, and produced an appearance which particularly attracted my notice, for I had never seen anything like it before, nor could I imagine who he was, nor what he came about. My doubts were, however, removed when Lord Hood introduced me to him. There was something irresistibly pleasing in his address and conversation, and an enthusiasm when speaking on professional subjects that showed he was no common being ... I found him ... singularly humane.[36]

The last word is revealing. It is the first independent reference to Nelson's humanity, which was an essential feature of his leadership. He had had many problems with the *Albemarle*, including issues of discipline – the log records some fifty floggings over the two-year period of his command, the severest being thirty-six lashes for desertion – but he had won the respect and loyalty of his men, whom he paternalistically referred to as 'my good fellows'. When the *Albemarle* returned to England and dropped anchor at Spithead on 25 June 1783, his junior officers and the whole crew pledged to join him immediately when he got another ship.

Peace came with the Treaty of Paris in September 1783. Britain lost its American colonies but retained its valuable sugar islands, which were destined to be Nelson's next posting. He had done well, strengthening his professional reputation for seamanship and combat. Notwithstanding serious bouts of malaria, he had also proved his physical resilience. He had no money, however, and in peacetime his immediate career path was unclear. This made the 24-year-old Nelson restless and desperate to do whatever he could to improve his standing in society. This goes a long way to explain his behaviour during the next phase of his life – behaviour which almost brought about an end to his naval career.

Without a ship to command, Nelson spent the first months of the peace in France trying with difficulty to learn the language and all too easily falling in love, not with 'French beauties', as he described them, but with Elizabeth 'Bess' Andrews, the young daughter of an English clergyman living in St-Omer. 'The critical moment of my life is now arrived, that either I am to be happy or miserable,' he wrote to his uncle, William Suckling, brother of Maurice, adding, 'It depends solely on you.'[37] He was asking for an allowance to boost his meagre income so that he would be able to propose. William agreed – but then Elizabeth refused him. Nelson returned to England in a forlorn mood; but he recovered from the blow to his pride when, in 1784, thanks to Lord Hood's influence, he secured a rare peacetime appointment. This saw him raise his flag on the 28-gun HMS *Boreas* and sail for the West Indies with orders to join Admiral Sir Richard Hughes as his second-in-command.

The posting proved an unhappy and controversial one. Hughes was lethargic. Nelson was zealous to protect the Leeward Islands and to secure British commerce. This included enforcing the Navigation Acts, which forbade ships from the newly independent America trading with the British islands. But it was not in the commercial self-interest of the governor of the Leeward Islands, or of the various merchants and traders on the islands, to prevent the illegal trade from continuing.

Driven by his strong and rigid sense of duty, Nelson proceeded to upset them all, taking several American ships and their cargoes as prizes. He would not compromise and even sought to teach his commander-in-chief his duty, to the point of copying his correspondence to the Admiralty. Nelson knew his actions would be popular at home, but his self-righteousness smacked of pride, arrogance and immaturity. When the government finally backed his stand it was Hughes who was congratulated for suppressing the illegal trade; Nelson's efforts were omitted from the official report. He determined to manage his own publicity in future. Meanwhile, angry merchants issued claims for damages against him, some of which were still being pursued many years later.

Nelson's troubles were not over even after Hughes had been recalled, leaving him as the senior officer on the station. A new set of challenges arose. The most serious was his handling of a delicate situation involving his new acquaintance, Prince William Henry, who had been given the command of the frigate *Pegasus*. The king hoped that service in the Royal Navy would temper his headstrong son. There was more than a touch of irony in the situation, given Nelson's insubordination to Admiral Hughes. Nelson's subsequent indulgence towards the prince, no doubt born of a natural wish to better his own place in society, dulled his usually acute sense of duty and impaired his better judgement.

The prince had been promoted beyond his abilities and experience. An older and highly competent first lieutenant, Isaac Schomberg, had been placed aboard by Hood to ensure the prince did not lose his ship. The prince, who knew this, frequently and unjustly dressed down Schomberg in front of fellow officers, typically over trifling matters. Rather than nipping this in the bud by having a quiet word with the prince, who was evidently impressed by Nelson's knowledge and conversation, he let things run until Schomberg could take no more. Schomberg demanded a court martial – at which point Nelson agreed to his request and placed him under arrest until the required number of post captains could be assembled for the trial. Consequently, the affair dragged on and the case developed into a major issue. The naive Nelson should have diffused the situation by pointing out the weakness of the prince's case and by asking Schomberg to withdraw his request for a court martial. This is what Commodore Alan Gardner did as soon as the *Pegasus* arrived some months later at Jamaica

But the damage was done. Lord Hood, the Admiralty and the king were displeased with Nelson. Whereas Prince William, by virtue of his rank, was little affected, Nelson suddenly found himself out in the cold. He professed in his 'Sketch of my Life', written in 1799, not to have understood why there was 'prejudice evidently against me at the Admiralty',[38] but in 1790 he had, in fact, received a letter from Hood stating clearly that the Schomberg affair was the reason for the Admiralty's disfavour. It would be five years 'on the beach' before the Admiralty called on Nelson to serve his country again.

From a personal rather than professional point of view, Nelson's time in the West Indies brought some joy, for it was here that he met his closest friend and future companion in arms, Cuthbert Collingwood. He also flirted with Mrs Moutray, the commissioner's wife, and met the amiable woman he would make his wife, the widow Frances Nisbet.

Collingwood, a reserved Northumbrian, was eight years older than Nelson and had been at sea since the age of 11. When Nelson left the *Lowestoffe*, it was Collingwood who filled the vacancy. In 1779, he was given command of the *Badger* brig, and followed in Nelson's footsteps again with promotion into the *Hinchinbroke* when Nelson shifted his flag to the 44-gun *Janus*. They finally met properly in the West Indies during the peace. Collingwood, in *Mediator*, and Nelson worked together to enforce the Navigation Acts. Collingwood had brought the Moutrays out from England and had formed a warm attachment to the intelligent, slender and vivacious Mrs Moutray by the time Nelson arrived. She soon captivated Nelson also. In the friendless 'hurricane hole' that was English Harbour – this 'vile place'[39] as Nelson referred to it – it was not long before he and Collingwood found themselves in love with the same woman. Nelson described her as 'a treasure of a woman'[40] and 'my dear, sweet amiable friend'.[41] She made him feel like 'an April day',[42] he said. Many years later, Collingwood recalled how she had allowed Nelson 'to frizzle your head for a ball dress at Antigua'.[43] Mrs Moutray cleverly kept both of her admirers at arm's length and they all exchanged letters and enjoyed friendship until their deaths. The Moutrays left Antigua in 1785. Writing to his brother William, Nelson pined:

> This country appears now intolerable, my dear friend being absent. It is barren indeed. Not all the Rosys can give a spark of joy to me. English Harbour I hate the sight of … By this time I hope she is safe in old England. Heaven's choicest blessing go with her.[44]

A few months later, Nelson visited the island of Nevis, where he met Frances Nisbet. She was a 24-year-old widow, considered 'pretty and attractive, and a general favourite'.[45] Known to everyone as Fanny, she had been born on the island. Her father was the senior judge and her uncle, John Herbert, was President of Council. She had married Dr Josiah Nisbet in 1779 and had moved to England, where she gave birth to a son, also named Josiah. In 1781, however, her husband died and she returned to Nevis to live with her uncle. What the mutual attraction was we may never know, but Prince William, writing to Hood, commented that 'Poor Nelson is over head and ears in love'.[46] Although John Herbert was one of those whose commercial interests were being threatened by Nelson, he appears to have liked the young man. He welcomed him into his house and was not dismayed at the increasing attention Nelson gave to his niece.

Nelson admired Fanny's accomplishments – she was fluent in French, painted watercolours and was an expert at embroidery. He wrote her affectionate letters during their courtship and continued to do so for a good while after they married. Six months before their wedding he penned:

My heart yearns to you, it is with you, my mind dwells with nought else but you. Absent from you, I feel no pleasure: it is you, my dearest Fanny, who are everything to me. Without you I care not for this world; for I have found lately nothing in it but vexation and trouble.[47]

This is a clear reference to being worn down by his peacetime responsibilities. He added:

These you are well convinced are my present sentiments: God Almighty grant they may never change. Nor do I think they will; indeed there is, as far as human knowledge can judge a moral certainty they cannot; for it must be real affection that brings us together, not interest or compulsion which makes so many unhappy.[48]

In another letter, he describes how his 'love is founded on esteem, the only foundation that can make love last'.[49]

They eventually married at Montpelier, John Herbert's estate in Nevis, on 11 March 1787. The bride was given away by Prince William Henry, who insisted on playing a part, which must have pleased Nelson. In the letter to Hood that described Nelson as 'over head and ears in love', the prince nevertheless also wondered whether it would last: 'He is now in for it. I wish him well and happy, and that he may not repent the step he has taken.' He added, 'However, seriously my lord, he is in more need of a nurse than a wife. I do not really think he can live long.'[50]

Nelson was indeed worn out. He was eager to return to England with Fanny, in the hope that he would get a more congenial appointment that would allow him to recover. Seeking glory was not foremost in his mind at this time, but neither were the five years of unemployment that awaited him.

He spent them with Fanny, sharing the cramped parsonage house at Burnham Thorpe with his father. This was the first and only period of his life in which he lived for any length of time with Fanny. The bitter winters disagreed with her and she was often confined to bed, while Nelson, without the Admiralty's favour, became irritable. He immersed himself in farming and local gossip, as he began to contemplate an unheroic future. Nelson longed for children but Fanny failed to conceive. It appeared that his future would be barren as well as bleak.

5

The Mediterranean

I cannot, if I am in the field of glory, be kept out of sight: wherever there is anything to be done, there Providence is sure to direct my steps.

Horatio Nelson, 1797[51]

While Nelson sat brooding in the isolation of north Norfolk, events in Continental Europe were taking a violent course. Having supported the rebellious American colonies, the people of France, Spain and Holland were now applying the same principles to their own oppressive monarchies. In July 1789, a Paris mob stormed the Bastille and the aristocracy fled into exile. The émigrés appealed to Austria and Prussia to come to the aid of Louis XVI, who was forced by the revolutionary National Assembly to declare war on them. The Assembly was soon replaced by the more radical Convention, under which the French army won an early victory against the Prussians and entered Brussels. In 1792 the French monarchy was abolished and, on 21 January 1793, Louis was guillotined. The British government, outraged at this regicide, expelled the French ambassador to London. In response, the Convention declared war against Britain. Nelson was offered command of the 64-gun *Agamemnon* – and his third opportunity to become a hero.

The *Agamemnon* was to join the prestigious Mediterranean station under the command of Nelson's friend and mentor, Lord Hood. Nelson revelled in his new ship and declared himself a glory hunter: 'If it is a sin to covet glory, I am the most offending soul alive.'[52]

The 12-year-old *Agamemnon* was smaller than the standard 74-gun ship of the line and was considered old fashioned. She was, however, faster and more manoeuvrable than the larger vessels, and Nelson's skill and experience as a frigate captain got the most out of her. The smallest battleship in the fleet, she was given detached duties, which were ideally matched to Nelson's independent spirit. She was a happy ship, with many of her crew coming from Norfolk, or from the *Boreas* and *Hinchinbroke*. Nelson's letters home are full of praise for her. From the very beginning he demonstrated her capabilities and his own by chasing a squadron of French frigates through dangerous shoals off Cape Barfleur. Proud of himself, he began the habit of sending detailed reports of his actions to his superiors and to other influential people, saying that he would not mind if they circulated them, not least to the newspapers.

Hood's primary objective was to support the royalists holding out in Toulon and thus to prevent this important naval base falling into the hands of the revolutionaries. While Nelson was on detachment, Hood arranged to defend the town on the understanding that it would renounce the Republic and entrust its military installations to him. The republican army laid siege to Toulon for three months. A successful bombardment directed by a young artillery officer, Napoleon Bonaparte, eventually rendered the town indefensible. Hood, with his relatively weak force, arranged for the destruction of the French fleet, to avoid it falling into revolutionary hands, followed by evacuation.

Nelson's detachment had been ordered to sail to Naples, where he was to persuade Ferdinand IV, the King of Naples and Sicily, to provide 6,000 troops for the defence of Toulon. Nelson negotiated skilfully, securing 2,000 troops immediately as being better than 6,000 in two weeks' time. He declared his self-satisfaction, emphasising that he had acted without authority from Hood.

It was during this visit to Naples that Nelson met the cultivated 63-year-old Sir William Hamilton, British minister to the court of the Two Sicilies, and his renowned and beautiful second wife, 28-year-old Emma. The three took to each other immediately. As Nelson wrote to Fanny about Lady Hamilton, 'She is a young woman of amiable manners and who does honour to the station to which she is raised.'[53] He did not meet the Hamilton's again for another five years.

While Hood was still trying to defend Toulon, he detached Nelson again. Off Corsica, Nelson intercepted a small French squadron, including the 38-gun frigate *Melpomène*. There followed a ferocious four-hour exchange of fire. This hardened Nelson to battle, although a change in the wind persuaded him to break off the action and prevented him from capturing the French frigate. As the Frenchman had got the better of him, Nelson conferred with his fellow officers, looking for reassurance that he had made the right decision. His ability to confer was one of the most important facets of his leadership. Henceforth, he consulted with his officers before rather than after battle.

Following the loss of Toulon, the British needed to secure a base in the Mediterranean. Hood planned to take Corsica, which was close enough to Toulon for him to blockade the French port. The island had two strong points, at Bastia and Calvi. At Bastia, Nelson was involved in early skirmishes and personally led the soldiers and sailors ashore rather than relying on more junior officers. The guns of the *Agamemnon* bombarded the French batteries of Bastia during a three-month siege. Although the impatient Nelson was all for rushing the defences, this more traditional approach proved successful and the town eventually surrendered on 22 May 1794.

Bastia had revealed poor cooperation between the navy and the army. Thanks to Nelson, and the excellent relationship he struck up with Major General Sir Charles Stuart, the attack on Calvi was better conducted. Nelson was on shore for almost the whole time, sleeping close to Stuart in the advance batteries. At around seven o'clock on the morning of 12 July, he was wounded in the face by a shower of gravel thrown up from a parapet by French round shot. One of the stones hit his right eye and is believed to have detached his retina. 'I can clearly distinguish light from dark, but no object,'[54] he wrote, making light of it, even though it is now believed that the damage was serious and even life-threatening. It was not an unsightly wound, so Nelson never wore an eyepatch.

Following the capture of Corsica, Hood, for political reasons, was relieved of his command and his place on the Board of the Admiralty. This brought to an end any influence he had to help further Nelson's career. In his place, the less-distinguished and over-promoted Admiral William Hotham took command. Nelson soon became frustrated by Hotham's inaction and was openly critical of it. Then, at last, in March 1795 at the Battle of the Gulf of Genoa, he was involved in the first fleet action of his career. In sight of the enemy, he came alive and imagined a heroic death: 'Life with disgrace is dreadful. A glorious death is to be envied, and, if anything happens to me, recollect death is a debt we must all pay, and whether now or in a few years hence can be of little consequence.'[55]

As was by now typical, Nelson displayed an independent approach and put the *Agamemnon* against the biggest two-decker in the world, the French *Ça Ira*. Working in concert with Thomas Fremantle in the *Inconstant*, Nelson fought in close action for two hours, requiring seamanship of the highest standard, and did the *Ça Ira* serious damage. Nelson lost only seven men, whereas the French ship lost 110. She fell easy prey to the British when fighting resumed the following day. Nevertheless, Hotham discontinued the action, content with just two prizes. Nelson was furious. 'Had Lord Hood been there,' he wrote to Fanny, 'he would never have called us out of action but Hotham leaves nothing to chance.'[56]

Hotham brought the French fleet to battle again on 14 July at Hyères, once more displaying hesitation and a disinclination to take risks. On this occasion, Nelson was critical of the time Hotham wasted forming his fleet into line of battle: 'My disposition can't bear tame and slow measures. Sure I am, had I commanded our fleet on the 14th that either the whole French fleet would have graced my triumph, or I should have been in a confounded scrape.'[57]

It was a lesson that would directly influence his plan of attack at Trafalgar, as we can see from his memorandum before the battle:

Thinking it almost impossible to bring a fleet of forty sail of the line into a line of battle in variable winds, thick weather, and other circumstances which must occur; without such loss of time, that the opportunity would probably be lost of bringing the enemy to battle in such a manner as to make the business decisive, I have therefore made up my mind to keep the fleet in that position of sailing (with the exception of the first and second in command), that the order of sailing is to be the order of battle.[58]

Nelson was already beginning to think in terms of annihilating his enemy and of a victory so overwhelming that it would destroy their force irreversibly. In a letter to a friend he wrote, how 'much risque must be run to achieve great and brilliant actions. But Hotham adheres to the old adage: a bird in the hand is better far than two that in the bushes are.'[59] Cautious commanders like Hotham made annihilation impossible.

Promoted to the rank of commodore on 9 April 1796, Nelson again found himself detached from the main fleet, although this time with a small squadron. He had a busy year cruising off the north-west coast of Italy. His main task was to act in support of the Austrians, who were defending their Italian possessions against the French army, which was brilliantly led by General Napoleon Bonaparte. At last this gave Nelson the experience of independent command, allowing him to take important operational decisions himself. His exploits, which included establishing a tight blockade of French-held ports, harrying the French coastal supply route and even capturing Napoleon's siege train at Oneglia, plus various successful amphibious operations, earned him the nickname 'little brigadier'. His part in the capture of the islands of Elba and Capraia won the respect of the First Lord of the Admiralty, Earl Spencer, together with Admiral Sir John Jervis, Hotham's replacement as commander-in-chief in the Mediterranean, and Sir Gilbert Elliot, the Viceroy of Corsica. Elliot, in particular, became a close friend and long-term supporter.

At the time, Nelson felt that he deserved far more than their respect. He wrote to Fanny, family and friends accordingly. To the Reverend Dixon Hoste, the father of one of his own protégés, he wrote:

> None since Lord Howe's action [the battle in the Atlantic fought against the French in 1794 and known as the Glorious First of June] can lay claim equal to me, five actions in my ship, three at sea, two against the walls of Bastia, two sieges and three boat fights are my claim and annexed to the hardest service of any ship this war.[60]

This was hardly modest, but impressively true.

Notwithstanding Nelson's activity, Britain lost the campaign. When, in the autumn of 1796, Spain entered the war on the side of France, the British had little choice but to abandon Corsica and withdraw the fleet from the Mediterranean altogether. Nelson masterminded the evacuation from Elba. He was appalled at the Cabinet's decision, which he saw as Britain deserting its allies. For one moment, he even thought of staying behind and offering his services to the King of Naples, adding that 'desperate affairs require desperate remedies'.[61] Having thought twice, however, he sailed in February to join Admiral Sir John Jervis's fleet, based in the Tagus below Lisbon. He soon found himself in the battle that would become the turning point of his career.

6

Cape St Vincent

When I am without orders and unexpected occurrences arrive I shall always act as I think the honour and glory of my King and Country demand. But in case signals can neither be seen or perfectly understood, no captain can do very wrong if he places his ship alongside that of the enemy.

Horatio Nelson, October 1805[62]

On 13 February 1797 Nelson arrived in the Tagus. There, he reported having spotted a Spanish fleet, comprising seven three-deckers, two 80-gun and eighteen 74-gun ships, plus a dozen frigates. Sir John Jervis had only fifteen ships of the line, but these included six powerful three-deckers. He was excited rather than daunted by Nelson's news. He himself had once declared 'men, not ships, win battles'.

Jervis put to sea immediately and, on the morning of 14 February, in foggy weather, sighted the Spanish off Cape St Vincent heading for Cadiz in two loose formations. 'They loom like Beachy Head in a fog. By my soul they are thumpers,'[63] called Lieutenant Henry Edgell of the *Barfleur*, who had gone aloft to get a better view. Jervis formed a single line of battle, told his captains that 'a victory is very essential to England at this moment'[64] and sailed for the gap between the formations. Having split the enemy into two unequal groups, he ordered his own fleet to tack in order that he could attack the main formation from the rear and to windward by rolling up the ill-formed enemy as Hawke had done at Quiberon Bay. Captain Thomas Troubridge in *Culloden* led the vanguard.

Before the majority of his line had tacked in succession behind *Culloden*, the smaller Spanish formation commanded by Vice Admiral Moreno had disrupted the manoeuvre. On seeing this, Admiral Cordóba, commander of the fleet, ordered his own, larger squadron to bear up and attack the British rear. From his flagship *Victory,* 100-guns, Jervis ordered his rear division to tack to block this move, but the divisional flagship *Britannia* missed the signal. Seeing this, and without hesitation, Nelson decided to act. Dramatically, he wore his 74-gun ship, the *Captain,* out of the line – a quicker and safer manoeuvre than tacking – and sailed directly to support the British van, which by now had begun to catch up with the rearmost Spanish ships of the larger formation. The two rearmost ships, *Excellent* (commanded by Collingwood) and *Diadem,* copied this manoeuvre, while Nelson took station ahead of Captain Troubridge's *Culloden* and succeeded in turning the Spanish formation back onto its old course. Nelson steered across the van of the Spanish ships and headed directly for the fleet flagship, the 136-gun *Santissima Trinidad,* the largest ship in the world, with four decks. A fierce contest of gunnery began.

For a long time Nelson's act of leaving the line was described as disobedience, since it was not sanctioned by the fighting instructions. In theory it could have cost him his career. It is clear, however, that he was acting within the spirit of Jervis's orders, which is why after the battle Jervis welcomed him aboard *Victory* and showered him with professional praise.

A number of the Spanish ships suffered badly from the accurate and rapid British broadsides. Two of them, the *San Nicholas,* 80-guns, and the *San Josef,* 112-guns, collided in their attempt to escape the murderous fire. Nelson ordered the *Captain,* now badly mauled, to go alongside and he himself, in an act of conspicuous heroism, led one of the boarding parties. After hand-to-hand fighting, he seized the *San Nicholas.* Then from her decks he went on to board the larger *San Josef,* forcing her to strike her colours as well. Nothing quite like this had happened before; nor had a British flag officer led a boarding party in person since Sir Edward Howard in 1513. The fleet dubbed the feat 'Nelson's patent bridge for boarding first rates'.[65]

Nelson's daring quickly captured the public imagination. This was a glamorous heroism that the ordinary person could understand, but it relied on the gallantry and teamwork of his brother officers, which Nelson recognised. The *San Josef* and *San Nicholas* had already been severely damaged by four other British ships before Nelson boarded them. The instant response of Troubridge and Collingwood to his initiative to leave the line had also been essential to the outcome, which is why on the following day he wrote to thank them for their support and visited Collingwood aboard his badly damaged ship.

Nelson had played a crucial and unprecedented role in a remarkable victory and could enjoy his laurels. Yet his earlier lack of recognition still rankled. To make sure his actions were not overlooked this time, he sent his own account of the action to his former captain, William Locker, with the request that he arrange for it to be published in the newspapers. This rubbed against the idea of teamwork and upset some of his fellow captains. Although Nelson's official report to the First Lord of the Admiralty stated that it would be 'improper to distinguish one from the other', his very different unofficial account supplied to the press brought him great advantage. The story made him a national hero and he was created a Knight of the Bath. He relished designing his own coat of arms, though tellingly he included the figure of an ordinary sailor as one of the supporters, acknowledging the debt he owed to the men who served with him.

Jervis recognised Nelson's special gift for inspiring men. In May he posted the newly promoted rear admiral and his flag captain, Ralph Miller, to the 74-gun *Theseus*, which had arrived on station with a half-mutinous crew. This was a difficult time for the Royal Navy: the year 1797 would witness two mutinies in the home fleets at anchorages of Spithead and the Nore. Nelson's personal magic and humanity worked. Two weeks later a note was left on *Theseus*'s quarterdeck:

> Success attend Admiral Nelson. God Bless Captain Miller. We thank them for the officers they have placed over us. We are happy and comfortable and will shed every drop of blood in our veins to support them, and the name of the *Theseus* shall be immortalized as high as *Captain*'s. Ship's Company.[66]

This, at least, is the version quoted by Nelson. Once more he had massaged the story, for the original referred also to

Sir Robert Calder, one of the captains who been critical of Nelson's actions at the Battle of Cape St Vincent. The original also made no reference to the *Captain*.

Jervis, now Earl St Vincent, demonstrated his confidence in Nelson by giving him command of an inshore squadron to cover the remnants of the Spanish fleet which had taken refuge in Cadiz. At night they tried to harass Nelson's ships with gunboats. Nelson was again involved in desperate hand-to-hand fighting with sword and cutlass. His life was only saved by the intervention of his coxswain, John Sykes, who was badly wounded in the arm as he protected Nelson. As Nelson wrote to the Duke of Clarence, 'We got amongst them the other night and took their commander, and with as my friends are pleased to say some personal honour to myself.'[67] It was extraordinary that a rear admiral should risk his life in this way, but it was Nelson's way to lead from the front, knowing that it would also stiffen the resolve of potentially mutinous sailors. Nelson mentioned Sykes in his dispatch, an almost unheard-of honour for a seaman, and saw to it that he was promoted.

Hubris is a dangerous quality and Nelson, heady with victory, adulation and possibly a sense of invincibility, was about to succumb to it. Jervis, impressed by his actions at Elba and Capraia, dispatched Nelson with a small squadron to make 'a vigorous assault' on the port of Santa Cruz de Tenerife in the Canary Islands. Despite careful planning, two attempted landings at dawn on 22 July failed. Information from a Spanish deserter led Nelson's captains to believe that a third attempt would succeed.

Nelson agreed with them. He ignored the lesson from the Grand Turk Island action and on 24 July, with the element of surprise gone, led a night-time frontal assault against an alert, well-trained and well-led defence, organised by the governor Antonio Gutiérrez, knowing it to be, in his own words, 'a forlorn hope'. The British casualties exceeded those at the Battle of Cape St Vincent. Nelson, who decided to lead the third attack, was among them. As he was about to leap ashore, with the sword bequeathed to him by Suckling in his hand, he was hit in the upper right arm by a musket ball which shattered the bones and severed the brachial artery.

Those who made it ashore, among them Captain Troubridge, were surrounded and forced to surrender. They were treated humanely, however, and allowed to return to their ships – an act of chivalry which Nelson complimented in an exchange of letters with Gutiérrez, and with gratefully received gifts of beer, cheese and wine. The defeated British squadron sailed away on 27 July.

The seriously wounded Nelson had been taken back to *Theseus*, where he underwent the painful amputation of his arm (he recommended afterwards that surgeons heated their blades). He might not have reached the surgeons at all but for his 17-year-old stepson Josiah, with him in the boat, who promptly applied a life-saving tourniquet with his silk necktie. Although in severe pain, Nelson displayed his usual fortitude and was writing spidery letters with his left hand within twenty-four hours of the operation, the most important being one to his commander-in-chief, Earl St Vincent:

> I am become a burthen to my friends and useless to
> my country … When I leave your command I become
> dead to the world. I go hence, and am no more seen.
> I hope you will be able to give me a frigate, to convey
> the remains of my carcass to England.[68]

During the miserable voyage home and the weeks in
England that followed, with his wound causing great
pain and refusing to heal, Nelson was utterly depressed.
He was convinced that 'a left-handed admiral will never
again be considered useful'.[69] His pride had been badly
damaged. He also mourned, with a degree of guilt, the
loss of officers and friends killed at Santa Cruz, worrying
that his protégés, not least Josiah, would suffer without his
'interest'. 'The sooner I get to a very humble cottage the
better,' he wrote, 'and make room for a better man to serve
the state.'[70]

St Vincent saw things differently. He wrote to Nelson:
'Mortals cannot command success, you and your
companions have certainly deserved it, by the greatest
degree of heroism and perseverance that was ever
exhibited.'[71] Two of those words would have meant
something special to Nelson: heroism and perseverance.
His flagging spirits were also boosted by the public
adulation he now received. His name appeared regularly
in the newspapers; popular prints of his battle scenes went
on sale; and cities, including the City of London, offered
him their freedoms. By October he was writing eagerly to
St Vincent, 'The moment I am cured I shall offer myself
for service.'[72] He was adapting well to the shock of the loss

of his arm, which he saw as a fortune of war, even as God's will; but physically it was a different matter. One of the ligatures tied to a severed artery remained in the wound for close on six months, causing infection and pain. Usually, ligatures could be pulled away within a few weeks. The day it dropped away he was a new man. Everything that had happened since he joined the navy would very soon be regarded as an apprenticeship. The year 1797 was his 'Year of Destiny'[73] and his greatest triumphs were yet to come.

7

The Battle of the Nile

If I had been censured every time I have run my ship, or fleets under my command, into great danger, I should have long ago been out of the Service and never in the House of Peers.

Horatio Nelson, March 1805[74]

Nelson returned to active service in the spring of 1798, hoisting his flag aboard HMS *Vanguard*, 74-guns, at Spithead on 29 March. After rejoining St Vincent off Cadiz, he was ordered at once to enter the Mediterranean in command of a detached squadron, with the specific task of discovering the destination of a large French expeditionary force known to be assembling in Toulon. St Vincent recognised the importance of this command and knew that it called for special qualities of leadership. His most promising junior was an instinctive choice.

At the beginning of 1798, Napoleon Bonaparte, abandoning the hope of invading England (following a key English naval victory at Camperdown on 11 October 1797), persuaded the French government, the Directory, to give him command of an expedition to invade Egypt, the aim being to open the way for an overland attack on British trade in India. The Directory was relieved to keep him and his Army of Italy as far away from Paris as possible. With remarkable improvisation, an expedition with 35,000 troops in 400 transports, escorted by thirteen ships of the line and seven frigates, sailed from Toulon on 19 May 1798. Capturing Malta on the way, Napoleon easily defeated the Mameluke rulers of Egypt at the Battle of the Pyramids, bringing the country under French control by the end of July.

Nelson's first task was to discover the destination of the French expeditionary force, but disaster struck in the early hours of 21 May, when his flagship was dismasted in a gale. As his other ships did not suffer badly, this reflected poor seamanship, most likely by his young flag captain, Edward Berry. It could not have happened at a worse time, for the French had sailed the day before and passed by unseen while Nelson was carrying out repairs in a Sardinian bay. Having missed various opportunities to rendezvous with the frigates of his squadron, he was delighted to be joined by Troubridge with reinforcements from the Channel Fleet. He now had thirteen 74-gun ships of the line, a 50-gun ship and a brig – a major fleet to command for the first time.

But where was the enemy? His intelligence was imperfect, but the prevailing westerly winds led him to look east and to Egypt. Based only on a hunch, it took considerable nerve to take his fleet 800 miles away from the usual theatre of operations. If he were wrong, Napoleon's force would be free to play havoc in the western Mediterranean. Nelson's heart sank when he reached Alexandria on 28 June to find no trace of the French.

Nelson had in fact arrived ahead of them. The French sailed unseen into Alexandria the day after he sailed out of it. He went north before, at last, he received intelligence confirming his instinct. On 1 August he returned to Alexandria, to see the port crammed with French transports, but no men-of-war. Nelson then sailed 9 miles east, to the only other possible anchorage, Aboukir Bay, where he found the French fleet at anchor in a defensive line.

During the long and frustrating chase Nelson had been busy talking to his captains, whenever the weather and circumstances would permit, enthusing them with his aggressive determination to annihilate the enemy. His closest confidants were Thomas Troubridge and James Saumarez, whom he consulted frequently before relaying the key points to those not present, by means of the public order book. By 1 August he had agreed the essence of the attack, which removed the need for central control. The ships were to be at constant readiness for action: keeping in close order at all times, ready to anchor by the stern in case the French were discovered at rest, before concentrating on and overwhelming one section of the enemy line. His written instructions, dated 18 June, separated his fleet into three divisions, delegating responsibility for their direction to three divisional commanders, who were given new signalling arrangements. In large letters, inked boldly, he made his goal abundantly clear: 'The Destruction of the Enemy's Armament is the Sole Object.'

The French were sighted at 2.30 p.m. on 1 August. It would take at least two hours to get to them. Sunset was about four hours away and the bay was uncharted. The French commander-in-chief, Admiral Brueys, must have expected battle the following day, giving him time to tighten his line and to call back the men ashore. But Nelson did not hesitate. He had the weather gage (that is, the advantageous windward position) and swooped down on the weak vanguard of his enemy, without stopping to form his fleet into its order of battle, just as Hawke had done at Quiberon Bay. Before the battle had even begun, he hoisted what was to become his trademark signal: 'Engage the enemy more closely'. This time he did have surprise on his side.

Then came the reward for the way he had given independence of action to his captains. Captain Thomas Foley in *Goliath* spotted the anchor buoy of the leading French ship 240 yards ahead of her. Foley realised that if there was room for the Frenchman to swing on its anchor, there was room for his ship to sail between the anchored ship and the shoals without the risk of grounding. This would then place him behind the enemy line. He steered *Goliath* accordingly, and four successive captains followed his example. Nelson himself then doubled the French line, at the risk of friendly fire, by anchoring to the seaward of the third French ship. The French van was overwhelmed, while the rest of the English fleet worked its way down the length of the French line to concentrate on the centre, each ship anchoring opposite her respective opponent.

De Brueys' centre was made up of the 120-gun *L'Orient* and two 80-gun battleships. They inflicted the most damage on the British ships, especially the *Bellerophon* and *Majestic*, which between them accounted for over 40 per cent of British casualties at the battle. Superior British gunnery, however, did its deadly work, and six of the thirteen Frenchmen had struck their colours before midnight. The ships in the French rear could do nothing to aid their comrades since the wind was blowing directly down their line, rendering them helpless. De Brueys was mortally wounded, being virtually cut in two by round shot, but he refused to be taken below, saying 'A French admiral ought to die on his own quarterdeck.'[75] Soon afterwards, *L'Orient* caught fire. At about 10 p.m. her magazine exploded so loudly that it deafened onlookers. Blazing debris from the ship, ejected from the fireball, fell all around, causing havoc and setting ships from both fleets alight. A piece of mast that hit *Swiftsure* was large enough for Captain Hallowell to have a coffin made from it, which he later presented to Nelson. The explosion was the awesome climax of a battle which ended with the destruction of eleven out of the thirteen French battleships, plus two frigates. No British ship was lost. This was the annihilation which Nelson had so long sought. The 'butcher's bill' speaks of the carnage: the French suffered 5,235 killed and 3,705 captured; the British 218 killed and 677 wounded. As Nelson himself remarked, 'Victory is certainly not a name strong enough for such a scene as I have passed.'[76] Only two of the French ships escaped, one of them commanded by Rear Admiral Villeneuve, a man destined to face Nelson again – at Trafalgar.

Nelson was himself wounded at the height of the action, when a piece of langridge, or flying scrap iron, struck him on the right side of the forehead, tearing away a flap of skin that exposed his cranium and fell over his good eye. Blinded with blood, he at first thought it a mortal wound, 'I am killed,' he exclaimed. 'Remember me to my wife.'[77] He was carried below to the cockpit. In spite of being in intense pain, when the surgeon broke away from a sailor he was attending to, Nelson stopped him. 'No,' he said. 'I will take my turn with my brave fellow.'[78]

This is an authentic account, not a romantic later invention, and it rings true. Nelson always concerned himself with his sailors' physical needs, including health and hygiene, but also their spiritual and emotional wellbeing. He encouraged music and dancing, and any activities which could sustain morale. He obtained Bibles for their pastoral care. On one occasion, asked by a mother to deliver a last-minute note to her midshipman son on his first voyage, he requested her to kiss it, so that he might take the kiss to her son too. No wonder the seamen loved him for his humanity and fellow-feeling.

The Battle of the Nile is widely regarded as Nelson's finest. The absolute nature of the victory restored Britain's supremacy in the Mediterranean. It also galvanised opposition to France, leading to the formation of the Second Coalition. For the Royal Navy, it established a habit of victory. For the French navy, it was a psychological blow from which it never recovered. For Nelson, it elevated him from being famous to being a major celebrity. For the rest of his life he was known as the 'Hero of the Nile'. Showered with international awards and decorations, he was no longer one hero among many. He was *the* hero.

8

Naples

My character and good name are in my own keeping. Life with disgrace is dreadful. A glorious death is to be envied.

Horatio Nelson, 10 March 1795[79]

After the Battle of the Nile, Nelson took his battered fleet to Naples. It was a fateful decision and it led to the darkest episode in his career – one that has remained controversial ever since. 'Naples is a dangerous place,' wrote Nelson, full of 'fiddlers and poets, whores and scoundrels.'[80]

It was meant to be a short visit, while he himself recovered and while repairs were made to his ships. On 22 September 1798, as the fleet sailed into the beautiful bay shimmering under the shadow of the smoking Vesuvius, all of Naples erupted in joyous welcome. An armada of small boats put out from shore to welcome him. The air rang with 'Rule Britannia' and 'See the Conquering Hero'. Among the throng were King Ferdinand, Queen Carolina, and Sir William and Lady Hamilton. 'Come here, for God's sake, my dear friend, as soon as the service will permit you. A pleasant apartment is ready for you in my house, and Emma is looking out for the softest pillows to repose the few wearied limbs you have left,' wrote Sir William.[81] The intended short visit was to end up lasting nearly two years; but it was not only the Hamiltons' comforts or Emma's particular attractions which detained Nelson.

Unwisely, he became embroiled in Neapolitan politics. Queen Carolina, sister of the executed French queen Marie-Antoinette, was the real power in Naples; her husband was only interested in hunting and women. She was keen to embark on an aggressive foreign policy intended to provoke a French attack, in the hope that this would bring Austria into the war. Talkative, pious and astute, she seemed able to manipulate her friend Emma Hamilton to influence Sir William – and in turn Nelson. Apparently unaware that the queen and her policies were disliked, Nelson followed his orders to support Britain's allies in the war against France. He was, however, a mere child when it came to serious political intrigue. Unable to speak French or Italian, he relied on Emma to translate for him and suspected nothing could be amiss.

Thus he backed a (successful) Neapolitan assault on Rome. But one week later the French counterattacked, defeating Ferdinand's army and marching on Naples, where they proclaimed what they termed the Parthenopean Republic. With consummate skill Nelson evacuated the court, together with Sir William and Lady Hamilton, 600 expatriates and £2.5 million in treasure, to Palermo, Sicily. There he stayed for five months, living ashore, ostensibly as the best way of maintaining communication with the widely dispersed allied forces. His naive attachment to the queen may have had some hold over him. The company of the Hamiltons certainly did. He greatly enjoyed their entertainments – although his complex responsibilities covering the whole of the Mediterranean and the security of Sicily were always his priority.

Nelson had to contend with the threat of a French fleet of nineteen ships of the line, which the Directory had ordered into the Mediterranean. It presented him with a dilemma. By staying in Sicily he could control the central and eastern

Mediterranean against the French threat. Against this, the *lazzaroni* – the poorest street people, of which there were many in Naples – led by Cardinal Ruffo, were now rising up against the Parthenopean Republic in Naples. Nelson's recently reinforced fleet was in a position to tip the balance in their favour and to restore Ferdinand to the throne. The king gave him absolute authority to act.

On hearing that Ruffo's mob had concluded an armistice with the Republican rebels, Nelson sailed from Palermo to secure the surrender of the city's castles, believing he would be gone for eight days. Forty days later he was at Naples, having become embroiled in a maelstrom of misinformation and duplicity for which his experience as a professional sailor used to decisive action was of little help.

The rebels left the forts but, contrary to their expectations, Nelson annulled the truce and abrogated the surrender agreement, arguing that it was beyond the authority of the signatories. They were put into polaccas – three-masted sailing vessels – anchored under the guns of Nelson's ships. The principal rebels – about 100 of the approximately 8,000-strong force – were seized and conducted on board. There they were tried and sentenced to summary execution. Inevitably, Nelson was personally implicated.

The darkest incident was his handling of the trial and execution of the former admiral of the Neapolitan fleet, Prince Caracciolo. Caracciolo, like so many others, had detested the Bourbon king's rule and joined the Republican revolutionaries. He was found guilty by a Neapolitan court convened without witnesses, at Nelson's invitation, aboard the British flagship, the 80-gun *Foudroyant*. Caracciolo was found guilty and immediately sentenced to hang from the yardarm of the Neapolitan flagship, rather than awaiting the arrival and signature of the king. Nelson rejected his request to be shot rather than hanged, as befitted his rank, and he even denied his plea for a stay of execution to prepare himself for death. Two weeks later, Nelson was hosting a reception on the poop deck of the *Foudroyant* for the royal family and the Hamiltons when Carracciolo's bloated corpse floated past. The prince has haunted Nelson's reputation ever since.

Throughout this period, Nelson's health had been in steady decline, worn down by years of fighting and responsibility. He may also have been suffering prolonged concussion from his head wound. Some have suggested that this helps to explain his poor judgement at this time. He wished to return home, but his sense of responsibility held him in thrall to Queen Carolina. He put the strategic significance of the Kingdom of the Two Sicilies above Malta, in contravention of Admiralty orders. Even when he was finally recalled, he escorted Queen Carolina to Leghorn (modern-day Livorno) before relinquishing his ship. He then spent three months travelling home overland with the Hamiltons.

As far as the London Establishment was concerned, their new hero, beloved by the people, was also an embarrassment. Earl Spencer, the First Lord of the Admiralty, wrote brusquely: 'I believe I am joined in opinion by all your friends here, that you will be more likely to recover your health and strength in England than in an inactive situation at a foreign court, however pleasing the respect and gratitude shown to you for your services.'[82] Nelson complained that the letter, and especially the word 'inactive', caused him 'much pain'. He would have been hurt even more if he had had seen Earl St Vincent's comments to Evan Nepean: 'He is a partisan. His ship always in the most dreadful disorder, and never can become an officer fit to be placed where I am.'[83]

9

Emma

What must be my sensations at the idea of sleeping with you! It sets me on fire.

Horatio Nelson, 1800[84]

The other factor that tarnished Nelson's reputation was his love affair with Emma Hamilton. She did more than provide 'the softest pillows' for his wearied body, but the attraction between them was not instantaneous. At first Nelson was simply bemused. He wrote to Fanny that when Emma first came aboard *Vanguard* with the king and queen, clad à la Nelson with a dress embroidered with anchors, she immediately 'fell into my arms more dead than alive. Tears however soon set matters to rights … the scene was in its way affecting.'[85]

Emma (born Emily) Lyon, the daughter of a blacksmith on the Wirral peninsula, made wonderful use of her undoubted good looks and 'natural genius'[86] to further her station in life. She became first servant and then mistress to a number of gentlemen, including Charles Greville, Sir William Hamilton's nephew, until a contemptible arrangement between the two men saw her traded and packed off to Naples in 1786, aged 21. She duly became Sir William's mistress and, less predictably, in 1791, his wife.

As a consequence of her beauty, Emma was celebrated before Nelson met her. The portraitist George Romney painted her more than fifty times, and her 'attitudes' or *tableaux vivants* portraying classical mythology were a highlight of the Grand Tour. Goethe was among those captivated by her exotic and sensual talent.

Like Nelson, Emma was impetuous and impulsively affectionate. It is hardly surprising that in the heady atmosphere of adulation they fell for one another. She praised him. She nursed him back to health. She gave him emotional support. They shared danger together. In December 1798, during the evacuation of the royal family to Palermo, when a great storm made everyone seasick or terrified, Nelson was moved by the calm and courageous way Emma dispensed help and, in particular, how she cared for Queen Carolina's youngest child, who died in her arms. This was the moment that melted his heart. At last in January 1800, during a cruise to Malta, they slept together. Writing exactly one year later, Nelson exclaimed, 'Ah! Those were happy times; days of ease and nights of pleasure.'[87] Nelson and Emma had three children together: twin girls born in January 1801 and another girl in December 1803. Only one of the children, Horatia, survived.

Nelson had never encountered anything like the intimate pleasures he now enjoyed with Emma. This was not through inexperience, since he had had at least one mistress whilst married to Fanny – a far-from-secret relationship with Adelaide Correglia, an opera singer in Leghorn, who was described by Thomas Fremantle as Nelson's 'dolly'. But physical relations with Emma were very different from those he had experienced with Fanny. Letters to his 'beloved Emma' convey his intoxication. In 1800 he wrote:

Separated from all I hold dear in this world what is the use of living if indeed such an existence can be called so. No separation, no time, my only beloved Emma, can alter my love and affection for you … it only remains for us to regret which I do with the bitterest anguish that there are any obstacles to our being united in the closest ties of this world's rigid rules, as we are in those of real love. Continue only to love your faithful Nelson as he loves his Emma. You are my guide I submit to you, let me find all my fond heart hopes and wishes with the risk of my life. I have been faithful to my word never to partake of any amusement: or sleep on shore.[88]

Writing five years later, in March 1805, the passion was as powerful as ever:

The ship is just parting and I take the last moment to renew my assurances to my dearest beloved Emma of my eternal love affection and adoration. You are ever with me in Soul, your resemblance is never absent from my mind, and my own dearest Emma I hope very soon that I shall embrace the substantial part of you instead of the ideal that will I am sure give us both *real pleasure* and *exquisite happiness*.[89]

Ironically, the lovers were hardly ever alone, since they lived with Sir William in an affable *ménage à trois* until he died in 1803. It also appears that Nelson believed that Fanny would be as accepting of his affair with his 'guardian angel' as Sir William had been. Fanny, however, did not believe in the long-term nature of the relationship. Her last memories of her husband, only two years earlier, had been amongst the happiest of her marriage. Lady Spencer had observed them behaving as if they were newly-weds. Bewildered at the turn of events, Fanny now wrote:

> I love him. I would do anything in the world to convince him of my affection. I was truly sensible of my good fortune in having such a husband. Surely I have angered him – it was done unconsciously and without the least intention. I can truly say, my wish, my desire was to please him.[90]

This letter was to Nelson's prize agent and confidant, Alexander Davison. Notwithstanding Davison's reassurance that her husband's ardour for Emma would cool, Fanny forced Nelson to choose between them. Nelson's new daughter, Horatia, may well have been the deciding factor in his decision to stay with Emma, but at the time it troubled his conscience severely.

He agreed to give Fanny a generous financial settlement, providing she agreed never to see him again. She reluctantly accepted his terms but nevertheless remained devoted to him, and to his memory after his death, never allowing a bad word to be said against him. Shortly before she died in 1831, Fanny told her granddaughter, 'When you are older, little Fan, you may know what it is to have a broken heart.'[91]

10

Copenhagen

Time is everything; five minutes make the difference between victory and defeat.

Horatio Nelson, 1801[92]

After a rapturous overland journey with the Hamiltons, Nelson being met with dazzling adulation on his way through Austria and Germany, the 'Hero of the Nile' expected to be met at Hamburg by a British frigate, kitted out and ready to carry him victorious to England. But there was none. He wrote to the Admiralty. He waited. No ship came. Finally, the party was forced to make its own way back, landing at Great Yarmouth, where cheering crowds again received him as a conquering hero. No matter that his scandalous relationship with Emma was well known and indeed lampooned by the caricaturists, or that he was viewed in distinctly less favourable terms by some of his colleagues. Sir John Moore described Nelson 'as more like the prince at the opera than the conqueror of the Nile'.[93] His old friend, Earl St Vincent, wrote, 'poor man, devoured with vanity, weakness and folly strung with ribbons and medals.'[94]

The Admiralty's reservations about Nelson were so serious that, when a League of Armed Neutrality of the North was formed among the Baltic states, led by Russia, to stop Britain's vital trade in naval stores, it appointed him second-in-command of the fleet sent to break it up. The ageing Admiral Sir Hyde Parker was chosen as commander-in-chief. Parker was given orders to sail to Copenhagen to persuade the Danes to leave the league or else face the destruction of their fleet and dockyards; and then Parker was to attack the Russian fleet at Reval and Kronstadt.

The Danish fleet, complemented by forts and floating batteries, was anchored in front of the city, but it was disorganised and ill-prepared when Parker's fleet arrived. Parker did not attack immediately, which strained Nelson's patience. His commander-in-chief had not even informed him of his plans. The diffident Parker, nevertheless, eventually delegated the attack to Nelson and gave him twelve ships of the line for the job. It would be Nelson's battle after all.

Meanwhile, the Danes had strengthened their defences and removed the buoys marking the approach channels. Nelson chose to attack from the south and positioned his fleet accordingly, dining his captains the night before aboard his flagship, the 74-gun *Elephant*, in order to make his plans clear to them all. Soundings had been taken the night before along the middle ground, but the depth of water close to the Danish line was unknown, so Nelson believed it was impossible to repeat the doubling of the line so brilliantly achieved at the Battle of the Nile. It meant, however, that the effective range would be between 200 to 400 yards, not the 'pistol shot' of 25 yards or closer which Nelson desired for the British guns to do their deadly work.

The significance of the shoals struck home when, at 9.30 a.m. on 2 April 1801, the order came to attack. Three of his ships quickly ran aground – a quarter of his battle fleet lost at a stroke. Nelson responded immediately and decisively and, like a general on a battlefield, hailed new instructions to his captains as they came up. He had originally planned to draw up his fleet by the stern, right along the enemy's line. He now told each captain in turn where to drop their anchors, ensuring that he could still bring a concentration of firepower on the enemy rear and centre.

Meanwhile Parker, seeing three ships flying distress signals, misjudged the situation and, at about 1 p.m., ordered Nelson to break off the action. This would have been disastrous, since Nelson's damaged ships would have been forced to run the gauntlet of the enemy's van and the powerful Trekroner Fort battery which guarded the approach to Copenhagen. Nelson ignored Parker's signal. Whether the famous story of his disobedience is true or mythical, it has become central to the Nelson story. 'Damn the signal!' he is reputed to have declared. 'Take no notice of it, and hoist mine for closer action. That is the way I answer such signals.' Then he turned to his flag captain Foley and added, 'Foley, you know I have lost an eye, and have the right to be blind when I like, and damn me if I'll see that signal!'[95]

At the heart of the action Nelson could see that, although it had taken a lot longer than he had expected, the Danish centre was close to collapse. This would allow him to bring his vessels within range to bombard Copenhagen's arsenal. 'It is warm work and this day may be the last to any of us at a moment,' he declared. 'But mark you, I would not be elsewhere for thousands.'[96]

Soon afterwards, at about 2 p.m., Nelson made his third direct intervention. Whether out of humanity, as he claimed, or as a *ruse de guerre*, he dispatched a letter under a flag of truce to the Danish crown prince addressed, 'To the brothers of Englishmen, the Danes.' He praised their courage but offered to break off the action to prevent further loss of life, the casualties now amounting to about 1,000 per side. He added that, if resistance continued, he would 'set on fire all the batteries' and even bombard the city. The Danes agreed to a truce and Parker left Nelson to handle the armistice negotiations. Unbeknown to Nelson, the Danes had heard of the assassination of Tsar Paul I, the key advocate of the Armed Neutrality. This allowed them to agree to the British terms, sensing correctly that Russia would now withdraw from the league.

A relieved Parker gave Nelson command of the Baltic Fleet. Although Nelson readied himself to attack the Russians at Reval, his diplomatic skills had paved the way for reconciliation with them. After this, Nelson left for England, but not before issuing a farewell message to his officers and men thanking them for their kindness to him and praising their courage in battle.

Battle had yet again offered Nelson the chance to salvage his career. At Copenhagen his determination, speed of thought and resourcefulness had secured another major victory. It had also revealed his humanity. He returned home in early July 1801 with his professional reputation fully restored.

11

Trafalgar

Gentlemen, when the enemy is committed to a mistake we must not interrupt him too soon.

Horatio Nelson, 1799[97]

In 1802, after ten years of war, France and England agreed the Peace of Amiens. In the months leading up to it, Nelson had been given command in the Channel and was stationed at Deal in Kent, covering the port of Boulogne, where the French were preparing for invasion. Nelson eschewed a passive blockade and launched a number of attacks on the port which were bloodily repulsed by Admiral Latouche-Tréville. During the peace, which was short-lived, Nelson and the Hamiltons made an elaborate tour of towns and cities in the south of England, the Midlands and Wales. He was feted wherever he went.

Hostilities resumed in May 1803. Britain once again declared war on France. Nelson was given command of the prestigious Mediterranean Fleet. The Trafalgar campaign, designed to thwart Napoleon's plans to invade England, had begun. Nelson hoisted his flag as Vice Admiral of the Blue in HMS *Victory* on 18 May 1803. For the next two years he played 'cat and mouse with these fellows'[98], including the talented Latouche-Tréville. When the latter died in August 1804, command of his squadron at Toulon passed to the very different Admiral de Villeneuve. 'A tallish thin man, a very tranquil, placid English-looking'[99] French aristocrat, he had been promoted rapidly because of his willingness to serve the Republic – and he had been one of the few to escape Nelson at the Battle of the Nile.

Nelson now showed great skill, shrewdness and calmness, as well as a superb ability to manage a fleet at sea. He upheld the morale of his officers and crews, maintaining the fleet at peak fighting efficiency without recourse to dockyard refits. He played the role of diplomat with the many rulers and allies bordering the Mediterranean. He watched over the activities of pirates on the North African coast. Finally, he gathered intelligence from all quarters. He wrote an average of thirty letters each day, an extraordinary output. Earl St Vincent, full of such sharp criticism five years earlier, now saw in Nelson those 'habits of business not common to naval officers'.[100]

As a fighting admiral, Nelson had a rare ability to express the complexity of a naval battle in a manner that those serving under him could easily understand. Moreover, at a strategic level, Nelson did not visualise a battle as an end in itself, but as a means of achieving wider political and commercial aims. In this light, his pursuit of the combined fleets of France and Spain across the Atlantic in early 1805, which could have been seen as leaving his station, was not an error of judgement but a piece of strategic brilliance as well as fine seamanship. Nelson was using naval power to ensure that France could not reach out beyond the European mainland, preventing any attempt its fleets might make to command the oceans. In doing so, he was securing British trade with the rest of the world at a time when commerce with most of Europe was blocked by the war.

Nelson's pursuit of the combined fleet, which came to be known later as the 'Great Chase', took place when Villeneuve managed to slip out of Toulon with eleven ships of the line, eight frigates and thousands of soldiers. From there he successfully passed through the Straits of Gibraltar and, after joining up at Cadiz with six Spanish ships of the line under the command of Admiral Gravina, got clean away to the West Indies. The aim was diversionary: to threaten Britain's sugar islands before heading back to unite with French Atlantic fleets at Ferrol and Brest. This would allow the concentration of the combined fleets of France and its allies in the Channel to support Napoleon's invasion attempt.

Startled at the news of Nelson's pursuit and of his arrival in the West Indies, Villeneuve decided to return to Europe prematurely. Nelson managed to alert the Admiralty, which strengthened the Western Squadron protecting the approaches to the Channel. There, on 22 July, the twenty ships of the combined fleet ran into Admiral Calder in command of fourteen ships of the line. In a confused action in fog, the Spanish lost two ships. Although it was not a decisive action, and indeed Calder was censured as a result, it demoralised Villeneuve, who sailed back south and eventually to Cadiz. Calder's action had major significance. Contrary to popular belief, it was this battle, rather than the Battle of Trafalgar, that prevented the invasion of England.

The combined fleet of thirty-three ships in Cadiz still posed a considerable threat. Nelson, who had returned to England on 18 August, wondered whether his failure to engage the enemy over the past two years would be held against him. He was, however, recognised as the most successful admiral of the age and as the saviour of his country, which was gripped with invasion fever (unaware that Napoleon had already broken his invasion camp at Boulogne and marched his Grande Armée south to fight the Austrians and Russians). Nelson remarked that he had 'been set up for a *conjurer* and God knows they will very soon find out I am far from being one ... if I make one wrong guess the charm will be broken'.[101] Yet he relished the promise of a fleet of forty ships of the line, confident that with such a force he could comprehensively annihilate the combined fleet.

There followed a hectic twenty-five days, during which, for the first time, he lived happily under the same roof as Emma and his daughter Horatia, at Merton Place, the 'paradise' that Emma had found for them both. The day before Nelson left, bound for Cadiz, they went to the parish church to receive private communion and to exchange rings, the nearest they could get to a marriage ceremony, for, as he avowed, 'in the eyes of God you are my wife'.[102] 'At half-past ten', on the evening of 13 September, he 'drove from dear, dear Merton, where I left all which I hold dear in this world, to go to serve my king and country'.[103] He hoisted his flag once more in *Victory* at Spithead and sailed to Cadiz, arriving the day before his forty-seventh birthday.

Nelson faced the challenge before him with his typical blend of thoroughness and enthusiasm. His fleet had been assembled in a hurry, but he wasted no time moulding his captains into another 'band of brothers'. Only a third of the twenty-seven captains who fought at Trafalgar had served with Nelson before. Only six had commanded a ship of the line in battle. Seven had never been in a battle and only five had experience of a fleet action. Over the course of two consecutive dinners, Nelson began to work his magic.

The first, on 29 September, his birthday, was attended by the senior commanders. The following evening he was joined by his junior commanders. This was followed by a series of smaller gatherings during the days leading up to the battle. At them he explained his approach, what he referred to as the 'Nelson Touch'.[104] He visualised an approach in three columns almost at right angles to the enemy line to 'surprise and confound' them. 'They won't know what I am about. It will bring forward a pell mell battle, and that is what I want.'[105]

The French and Spanish admirals expected the English divisions to come together to form a line parallel to theirs, but it was Nelson's intention to drive aggressively, with his largest ships leading, through the enemy line in three places. This would bring overwhelming force against their centre and rear, crushing them as quickly as possible, before their van could come about and join in the battle. In this way he would bring about annihilation. In making this purpose of the battle clear to his captains, he said, 'We can have only one great objective in view, that of annihilating our enemies, and getting a glorious peace for our country.'[106] As a principle, he reminded his captains that 'in case signals can neither be seen or perfectly understood, no captain can do very wrong if he places his ship alongside that of an enemy'.[107]

Nelson remained in charge, but he had empowered his subordinates. His captains were in awe. 'I dined with his Lordship yesterday,' wrote George Duff, 'and had a very merry dinner; he is certainly the pleasantest admiral I ever served under.'[108] He added in another letter, 'He is so good and pleasant a man, that we all wish to do what he likes, without any kind of orders.'[109] Captain Edward Codrington agreed: 'even you, our good wives, will allow the superiority of Lord Nelson in all these social arrangements which bind his captains to their admiral.'[110]

The combined fleet came out of Cadiz on 19 October, heading for the Mediterranean. Nelson, who had kept his main force about 50 miles out to sea, used a chain of frigates to shadow Villeneuve until the French admiral was well clear of Cadiz. According to Hercules Robinson, aboard the frigate *Euryalus*, it was 'a beautiful misty sun-shiny morning' as the sun rose above the white cliffs of Cape Trafalgar.[111] The combined fleet came into view at about 6 a.m. on Monday, 21 October 1805. Because his task force was still only twenty-seven ships, rather than the forty he had hoped for, Nelson ordered the British fleet to form two rather than three divisions, with the order of sailing being the order of battle. He led the weather division and Vice Admiral Cuthbert Collingwood, his friend and second-in-command, led the lee division.

With very little wind, it took nearly six hours at an agonisingly slow speed of 2 knots before the fleets clashed. This gave Nelson time to write to his 'dearly beloved Emma'; to add a codicil to his will leaving her and his daughter Horatia to the care of nation; to write a remarkable prayer; and to send a famous signal. His prayer is regarded as among the finest written by any soldier or sailor about to go into battle and is 'truly characteristic of the Christian hero':

May the Great God whom I worship grant to my country and for the benefit of Europe in general a great and Glorious Victory; and may no misconduct in anyone tarnish it, and may humanity after victory be the predominant feature in the British Fleet. For myself individually I commit my life to Him who made me, and may His blessing light upon my endeavours for serving my country faithfully. To Him I resign myself and the just cause which is entrusted to me to defend. Amen. Amen. Amen.[112]

At 11.25 a.m. he sent out the message 'England expects that every man will do his duty'. He had wanted to use the word 'confides' rather than 'expects' – he had confidence in everyone: it was a subtle but important Nelsonian difference. However, as it would have used more flags and taken longer to hoist, he accepted the word change. On seeing the signal, Collingwood gave the impression that he was irritated by it. 'What is Nelson signalling about?' he exclaimed. 'We all know what we have to do.'[113] But, once he grasped the signal's meaning, 'he expressed great delight and admiration'.[114] Everyone was clear about Nelson's plan; they all knew what they had to do.

Nelson's last signal was 'Engage the enemy more closely'. This was what, as he delightedly exclaimed, 'that noble fellow'[115] Collingwood was doing. Collingwood's division was the first to engage and it enveloped the enemy's. Meanwhile, Nelson's tactical mind was active. How could he hold down the enemy's van with fewer ships in his fleet than he had planned for in his memorandum and with only two columns as opposed to three? His eleven ships had to do the work of the weather column and the missing division. He had to improvise. So he led his ships towards the van to hold it in place. It was a feint. At the last minute he ordered *Victory* to turn to starboard, pointing her at the centre of the enemy line, cutting it astern of Villeneuve's flagship, *Bucentaure*, and doing terrible damage to her.

Victory soon found herself in a duel with the French *Redoubtable*. It was from the latter's rigging that a sharpshooter fired the musket ball which mortally wounded Nelson. It was not an aimed shot. There was too much smoke for that, and the intensity of the French musketry was already felling those on *Victory*'s upper decks before Nelson himself was hit. He was carried down to the cockpit below the waterline and struggled in great pain to stay in command until he knew he had won a decisive victory. His last hours were carefully recorded. He did say 'Kiss me Hardy' to his old friend and flag captain, Thomas Hardy. Hardy did so and then knelt and kissed him again in a gesture of sad farewell. He was not present when Nelson died. The final coherent words he uttered were, 'Now I am satisfied. Thank God I have done my duty.' His very last words were, 'Drink, drink. Fan, fan. Rub, rub.'[116]

The Battle of Trafalgar raged for less than five hours. Only a third of the French and Spanish ships facing Nelson on that day managed to escape capture or destruction. The British lost 450 men killed and 1,250 wounded, while the allies suffered more than 4,400 killed and 3,300 wounded. Many more were drowned during the storm which followed the battle. The British had not lost a single ship. But their most celebrated naval leader was dead. George III expressed the feelings of many of his people when he said, 'we have lost more than we have gained.'[117]

12

Immortal Memory

Thus it may be exemplified by my life that perseverance in any profession will most probably meet its reward.

Horatio Nelson, 1799[118]

Writing to his fiancée, Mary Gibson, after the Battle of Trafalgar, Captain Francis Austen, the brother of Jane Austen, sought to explain the essence of Nelson's remarkable personality:

> I never heard his equal, nor do I expect again to see such a man. To the soundest judgement he united prompt decision and speedy execution of plans; and he possessed in superior degree the happy talent of making every class of persons pleased with their situation and eager and happy to exert themselves in forwarding the public service.[119]

Meanwhile, Nelson's close friend, the Reverend Alexander Scott, also writing after the battle, described how Nelson's personality could lead to the closest affection:

> Men are not always themselves and put on their behaviour with their clothes, but if you live with a man on board ship for years, if you are continually with him in his cabin, your mind will soon find out how to appreciate him. I could forever tell of the qualities of this beloved man, Horatio Nelson. I have not shed a tear before the 21st October,

and since whenever I am alone, I am quite like a child.'[120]

He added, 'when I think, setting aside his greatness, what an affectionate, fascinating little fellow he was, how kind and condescending his manners, I become stupid with grief for what I have lost.'[121]

This strength of feeling was not reserved for those who knew Nelson personally. In the words of Lord Malmesbury, 'He added to genius, valour and energy, the singular power of electrifying all within his atmosphere and making them only minor constellations to his most luminous planet … it was his art to make all under him love him, and own his superiority without a ray of jealousy.'[122] When the people of Britain heard of Nelson's death, they reacted as if they had lost a dear and close friend. The outpouring of grief across the nation was extraordinary and widespread. His death overshadowed the news of the victory.

Nelson was given a spectacular five-day heraldic funeral, the last of its kind in Britain, but also the first state funeral for a man born a commoner. After lying in state, and a river-borne funeral procession, the coffin was escorted by thirty-two admirals, over 100 captains and 10,000 soldiers through huge crowds to St Paul's Cathedral, where he now lies in the crypt.

Sir Isaac Heard, Garter King at Arms at the Heralds' Office, was responsible for all of the complex arrangements, but when the public heard that he had excluded sailors from *Victory* from the ceremony there was uproar and he allowed forty-eight of them to escort the coffin. They stole the show. As the coffin was slowly lowered on a specially built mechanism into the torch-lit crypt, they were required to fold the shot-torn colours reverently and place them on the coffin as it disappeared from view. Quite unexpectedly, they suddenly tore off a large piece and ripped it into fragments which they stuffed into their jackets. The marvellous spontaneity of the moment caught everyone's breath, and the wife of Captain Edward Codrington of the *Orion* expressed its meaning perfectly: 'That was *Nelson*: the rest was so much the Herald's Office.'[123]

Nelson was immortalised by artists, writers and poets alike. The lustre they burnished has never really ceased to shine, not even after more than 200 years. Nelson remains the most popular British hero in history. Every year the Royal Navy and other institutions toast the Immortal Memory on the anniversary of his death. He is revered by navies around the world because he is seen as the embodiment of virtues which provide an enduring model for professional naval leaders.

Our intimate understanding of Nelson, which comes from the massive amount of correspondence he left behind, together with the writings of his peers and contemporaries, reveals the man in all his moods. As a result he seems familiar to us and so belongs as much to the present as to the past.

Very few people deliberately set out to become a hero as Nelson did. It was a lofty ambition. Nelson believed in himself, persevered and achieved his goal, going further than even he must have thought possible. He breathed into the Royal Navy his own ardour and his own ambition. In a few short years he revolutionised not only sea warfare but the very concept of victory. In doing so, he achieved a unique standing amongst sailors. 'Nelson brought heroism into the line of duty. Verily he is a terrible ancestor.'[124]

On Nelson's death, Fanny received a pension for life. Emma received nothing, in spite of Nelson's clearly expressed wish that she should become 'a legacy to my king and country, that they will give her an ample provision to maintain her rank in life'.[125] Emma died destitute in Calais in January 1815, the year of Waterloo. Even the last wishes of the greatest of heroes can be ignored, which says more about those who celebrate them than the heroes themselves.

Notes

1   Nicolas, Nicholas Harris, *The Dispatches and Letters of Vice Admiral Lord Viscount Nelson*, vol. 4 (1845) p. 487.

2   White, Colin, *1797: Nelson's Year of Destiny* (1998) p. 133.

3   Sugden, John, *Nelson: A Dream of Glory* (2004), p. 356.

4   Nicolas, Nicholas Harris, *Dispatches and Letters of Lord Nelson*, 7 vols (1884–7), vol. 1, 'Sketch of my Life', p. 15.

5   Hibbert, Christopher, *Waterloo: Napoleon's Last Campaign* (1967) p. 224.

6   Nicolas, *Dispatches and Letters of Lord Nelson*, vol. 7, p. 92.

7   Pettigrew, Thomas, *Memoirs of the Life of Admiral Lord Viscount Nelson*, 2 vols (1849), vol. 2, p. 428.

8   Ibid., vol. 2, p. 462.

9   Harrison, James, *Life of the Rt Honourable Horatio, Lord Viscount Nelson* (1806), pp. 8–9.

10 Sugden, *Nelson: A Dream of Glory*, p. 32.

11 White, Colin, *The Nelson Encyclopaedia* (2002), p. 121.

12 Clarke, J.S. & McArthur, J., *The Life of Admiral Lord Nelson KB*, 2 vols (1809), vol. 1, pp. 13–15.

13 Ibid.

14 Ibid.

15 Ibid.

16 White, *The Nelson Encyclopaedia* (2002), p. 213.

17 Pettigrew, Thomas, *Memoirs of the Life of Vice-Admiral Lord Viscount Nelson K.B.* vol. 2 (1849), p. 580.

18 Nicolas, *Dispatches and Letters of Lord Nelson*, vol. 1, p. 2.

19 Ibid.

20 Savours, Ann, 'A Very Interesting Point in Geography: The 1773 Phipps Expedition towards the North Pole', *Arctic* (1984), p. 418.

21 Ibid., p. 74.
22 Clarke & McArthur, *Life of Admiral Lord Nelson KB*, vol. 1, p. 23.
23 White, *The Nelson Encyclopaedia*, p. 166.
24 Sugden, *Nelson: A Dream of Glory*, p. 181.
25 Sugden, *Nelson: A Dream of Glory*, p. 576.
26 Slope, Nick, *The Life of Admiral Lord Nelson* (2010) p. 10.
27 Knight, Roger, *The Pursuit of Victory: The Life and Achievements of Horatio Nelson* (2005), p. 61.
28 Ibid., p. 63.
29 Sugden, *Nelson: A Dream of Glory*, p. 271.
30 Ibid., p. 195.
31 White, Colin (ed.), *Nelson: The New Letters* (2005), p. 136.
32 Ibid., p. 140.
33 Sugden, *Nelson: A Dream of Glory*, p. 213.
34 Nicolas, *Dispatches and Letters of Lord Nelson*, vol. 2, p. 346.
35 Clarke & McArthur, *Life of Admiral Lord Nelson KB*, vol. 1, pp. 78–9.
36 Sugden, *Nelson: A Dream of Glory*, pp. 215–16.
37 Ibid., p. 240.
38 Nicolas, *Dispatches and Letters of Lord Nelson*, vol. 1, p. 5.
39 Naish, G.P.B. (ed.) *Nelson's Letters to his Wife and Other Documents, 1785–1831* (1958), p. 19.
40 White, *The Nelson Encyclopaedia*, p. 179.
41 Ibid.
42 Sugden, *Nelson: A Dream of Glory*, p. 278.
43 Ibid., p. 281.
44 Ibid., p. 279.
45 Ibid., p. 311.
46 Knight, *The Pursuit of Victory*, p. 114.
47 Naish, *Nelson's Letters to his Wife*, p. 19.
48 Ibid.
49 Sugden, *Nelson: A Dream of Glory*, p. 349.
50 Knight, *The Pursuit of Victory*, p. 114.

51 Nicolas, *Dispatches and Letters of Lord Nelson*, vol. 2, p. 230

52 Ibid., p. 129.

53 Naish, *Nelson's Letters to his Wife*, p. 91.

54 Sugden, *Nelson: A Dream of Glory*, p. 510.

55 Naish, *Nelson's Letters to his Wife*, p. 97.

56 Ibid., p. 216.

57 Ibid.

58 White, *The Nelson Encyclopaedia*, p. 271.

59 White, *Nelson: The New Letters*, p. 165.

60 Ibid., p. 156.

61 Ibid., p. 165.

62 Nicolas, *Dispatches and Letters of Lord Nelson*, vol. 7, p. 91.

63 Sugden, *Nelson: A Dream of Glory*, p. 689.

64 Ibid.

65 Nicolas, *Dispatches and Letters of Lord Nelson*, vol. 1, p. 339.

66 Clarke & McArthur, *Life of Admiral Lord Nelson KB*, vol. 2, p .19.

67 Naish, *Nelson's Letters to his Wife*, p. 326.

68 White, *1797: Nelson's Year of Destiny*, p. 129.

69 Nicolas, *Dispatches and Letters of Lord Nelson*, vol. 2, p. 435.

70 Ibid.

71 Clarke & McArthur, *Life of Admiral Lord Nelson KB*, vol. 3, p. 61

72 Nicolas, *Dispatches and Letters of Lord Nelson*, vol. 2, p. 448.

73 The description 'Year of Destiny' was coined by Colin White.

74 Mahan, Alfred Thayer, *The Life of Nelson: The Embodiment of the Sea Power of Great Britain* vol. 1 (1897), p. 19.

75 Gardner, Robert, *Nelson against Napoleon* (2004), p. 35.

76 Sugden, John, *Nelson: The Sword of Albion* (2012), p. 106.

77 Ibid., p. 95.

78 Nicolas, *Dispatches and Letters of Lord Nelson*, vol. 3, p. 55.

79 Mahan, *The Life of Nelson: The Embodiment of the Sea Power of Great Britain*, vol. 1 (1897), p. 173.

80 Lowry, James, *Fiddlers and Whores: The Candid Memoirs of a Surgeon in Nelson's Fleet* (2006) p. 3.

81 Sugden, *Nelson: The Sword of Albion*, p. 124.

82 Coleman, Terry, *Nelson: The Man and the Legend* (revised edition, 2002), p. 231.

83 Ibid., p. 356.

84 Sugden, *Nelson: The Sword of Albion*, p. 402.

85 Knight, *The Pursuit of Victory*, p. 310.

86 Knight, Cornelia, *Autobiography of Miss Cornelia Knight* (1861) p. 310.

87 Knight, *The Pursuit of Victory*, p. 339.

88 White, *Nelson: The New Letters*, p. 43.

89 Ibid., p. 49.

90 Ibid., p. 41.

91 Hibbert, Christopher, *Nelson: A Personal History* (1994), p. 409.

92 Keane, Michael, *Dictionary of Modern Strategy and Tactics* (2005), p. 204.

93 White, *Nelson: The New Letters*, p. 43.

94 Warner, Oliver, *Nelson's Last Diary* (1960), pp. 61–67.

95 Coleman, Terry, *The Nelson Touch: The Life and Legend of Horatio Nelson* (2004) p. 223.

96 Sugden, *Nelson: The Sword of Albion*, p. 441.

97 Wescott Allan, *Mahan on Naval Strategy: Selections from the Writings of Rear Admiral Alfred Thayer Mahan* (1941) p. 267.

98 Nicolas, *Dispatches and Letters of Lord Nelson*, vol. 7, p. 92.

99 Robinson, Hercules, *Sea Drift* (1858), p. 208.

100 Coleman, *Nelson: The Man and the Legend*, p. 259.

101 Southey, Robert, *The Life of Horatio Lord Nelson*, (1828) p. 47.

102 White, *Nelson: The New Letters*, p. 48.

103 Ibid., p. 439.

104 Coleman, *The Nelson Touch*, p. 315.

105 Nicolas, *Dispatches and Letters of Lord Nelson*, vol. 7, p. 60.

106 Jones, S. & J. Gosling, *Nelson's Way: Leadership Lessons from the Great Commander* (2011) p. 188.

107 Nicolas, *Dispatches and Letters of Lord Nelson*, vol. 7, pp. 89–92.

108 Ibid., pp. 89–95.

109 Sugden, *Nelson: The Sword of Albion*, p. 505.

110 Ibid.

111 Codrington, Edward, *Memoir of the Life of Admiral Sir Edward Codrington* (1873) p. 51.

112 Warwick, Peter, *Tales from the Front Line: Trafalgar* (2012), p. 118.

113 Nicolas, *Dispatches and Letters of Lord Nelson*, vol. 7, pp. 139–40.

114 Collingwood, G.L. Newnham: *A selection from the public and private correspondence of Vice-Admiral Lord Collingwood* (1828) p. 125

115 Lambert, Andrew, *Nelson, Britannia's God of War* (2004), p. 295.

116 Ibid., p. 296; Beatty, William, *The Authentic Narrative of the Death of Lord Nelson* (1807), p. 42.

117 Hibbert, *Nelson: A Personal History*, p. 381.

118 Nicolas, Dispatches and Letters of Lord Nelson, vol. 1, p. 15

119 Warwick, *Tales from the Front Line*, p. 41.

120 Adkin, Mark, *The Trafalgar Companion* (2005), p. 17.

121 Ibid.

122 Lord Malmesbury, *Diaries and Correspondence of James Harris, First Earl of Malmesbury*, 4 vols (1844) vol. 4, p. 311.

123 Lady Bourchier ed. *Memoir of the life of Admiral Sir Edward Codrington* (1875).

124 Conrad, Joseph, *Mirror of the Sea* (1906), ch. 47.

125 Nicolas, *Dispatches and Letters of Lord Nelson*, vol. 7, p. 141.

Timeline

1758	29 September: Born Burnham Thorpe, Norfolk
1767	26 December: Death of Nelson's mother
1771	March: Joins the *Raisonnable* as a midshipman
	Voyage to West Indies in a merchantman
1773	Joins expedition to the Arctic
	Joins *Seahorse* and voyage to East Indies
1775	Invalided home with malaria
	Start of American War of Independence
1777	April: Passes for lieutenant
	Joins *Lowestoffe* and sails to West Indies
1778	Promoted commander of the armed brig *Badger*
1779	Promoted to post captain in *Hinchinbroke*
1780	Naval commander of San Juan River expedition
	Returns sick to England
1781	Appointed captain of *Albemarle*, North Sea
1782	Joins North American squadron and visits
	Quebec and West Indies
1783	End of American War of Independence
	Visits France
1784	Appointed captain of the frigate *Boreas* and sails
	to West Indies
1785	Meets Frances Nisbet
1786	Appointed aide-de-camp to Prince William Henry
1787	11 March: Marries Frances Nisbet on Nevis
	Boreas paid off
	Spends next five years at Burnham Thorpe on
	half pay

1789	French Revolution
1793	Louis XVI executed; French Revolutionary War starts
	26 January: Appointed to command *Agamemnon*
	Serves in Mediterranean and meets Sir William and Lady Hamilton at Naples
1794	12 July: Loses sight in right eye at Calvi, Corsica
1795	14 March: *Agamemnon* in action against *Ça Ira*
1796	Appointed commodore; hoists flag aboard *Captain*
1797	14 February: Battle of Cape St Vincent
	Knighted and promoted Rear Admiral of the Blue
	24 July: Loses right arm in attack on Santa Cruz de Tenerife
	Returns to England to recover
1798	1 August: Battle of the Nile
	Created Baron Nelson of the Nile and Burnham Thorpe
	December: Rescues Neapolitan royal family; Naples seized by French
1799	Promoted Rear Admiral of the Red
	Supports royalist recapture of Naples and orders the execution of Prince Caracciolo
	Created Duke of Brontë by King of Naples
1800	Recalled to England and makes overland journey via Vienna with the Hamiltons
1801	Promoted Vice Admiral of the Blue
	Separates from wife; birth of daughter Horatia
	2 April: Battle of Copenhagen
	Created Viscount Nelson
	15 October: Failed attack on Boulogne

1802	Peace of Amiens
	Tours South Wales and Midlands with the Hamiltons
	26 April: Nelson's father dies
1803	6 April: Sir William Hamilton dies
	16 May: Start of Napoleonic War
	Nelson appointed commander-in-chief in the Mediterranean and joins *Victory*
1805	April to July: Pursuit of combined fleet to West Indies and back
	21 October: Battle of Trafalgar; Nelson killed in action
1806	5–9 January: Lying and state followed by funeral service and interment in St Paul's Cathedral